Laura
(212) 586-2344

A Choice of Anglo-Saxon Verse

A Choice of
Anglo-Saxon Verse

*Selected, with an introduction
and a parallel verse translation by*

RICHARD HAMER

FABER AND FABER LIMITED
3 QUEEN SQUARE
LONDON

First published in 1970
by Faber and Faber Limited
3 Queen Square London WC1
Reprinted 1972 and 1974
Printed in Great Britain by
R. MacLehose and Company Limited
The University Press Glasgow
All rights reserved

ISBN 0 571 08765 5 (Faber Paper Covered Editions)

ISBN 0 571 08764 7 (Hard bound edition)

Metre in circled poems.

Contents

7

CONTENTS

8

Preface

The intention of this book is to make available a wide range of the shorter Old English poems with a parallel verse translation. All the most famous short poems are included. The apparatus is intended to give the minimum necessary information to those with little or no previous knowledge of the subject, except that I have given some notes designed to give some idea of the kind of problems that have to be grappled with by the editors in dealing with textual problems. I have throughout been greatly in the debt of the editors and commentators of the past, and I hope the extent of my debt has been made adequately apparent in the brief bibliographies and in my references.

Apart from this general debt I should like to express my thanks in particular for permission to print verbatim the texts of some of the poems from various editions: to Raytheon Education Company of Boston, Ma., for 'The Fight at Finnsburh' from *Beowulf And The Fight At Finnsburg*, F. Klaeber ed., D. C. Heath and Company: Boston, 1950; to the author and William Heinemann Ltd. for the text from A. Campbell, *The Battle of Brunanburh*, London, 1938; and to Columbia University Press for permission to quote from G. P. Krapp and E. V. K. Dobbie, *The Anglo-Saxon Poetic Records*, 6 vols., New York, 1931–53, as follows: *Durham*, vol. 6, p. 27, *Wulf and Eadwacer*, vol. 3, pp. 179–80, *Charm 12*, vol. 6, p. 128, *Almsgiving*, vol. 3, p. 223, *The Metrical Preface* and *Epilogue to the Pastoral Care*, vol. 6, pp. 110–12, *The Whale*, vol. 3, pp. 171–4, and the quotation from *The Fortunes of Men* on p. 88, vol. 3, p. 155; and for permission within the British area to George G. Harrap and Co. Ltd. for 'The Fight at Finnsburh' and to Routledge and Kegan Paul Ltd. for the

9

poems listed above from *The Anglo-Saxon Poetic Records*. In using these texts I have marked vowel length where it was not already done, and have made some minor alterations in punctuation. Apart from these poems my texts are the result of my comparison of earlier editions, and I owe a debt in particular to Sweet's *Anglo-Saxon Reader*, of which I have used the editions of both C. T. Onions and D. Whitelock, to J. C. Pope, *The Rhythm of Beowulf*, Yale, 1966, to R. F. Leslie, *Three Old English Elegies*, Manchester, 1961, and to the editors of the poems here used which have appeared in Methuen's Old English Library. I am also grateful to Mr. I. C. Butler who has suggested many improvements in the translations, and to Mr. C. J. E. Ball for much advice on the apparatus. As this help was given at an early stage of the composition of the book, neither of them is to blame for such defects as are to be found in its final form.

Abbreviations

ASPR *Anglo-Saxon Poetic Records*, in six volumes, published by Columbia University Press, containing the entire corpus of extant Old English poetry with invaluable apparatus. The following four entries give details of the volumes used.

ASPR II G. P. Krapp, *The Vercelli Book*, 1932.

ASPR III G. P. Krapp and E. V. K. Dobbie, *The Exeter Book*, 1936.

ASPR IV E. V. K. Dobbie, *Beowulf and Judith*, 1953.

ASPR VI E. V. K. Dobbie, *The Anglo-Saxon Minor Poems*, 1942.

EETS Early English Text Society.

Kershaw N. Kershaw, *Anglo-Saxon and Norse Poems*, Cambridge, 1922.

Pope, 7 OE P. J. C. Pope, *Seven Old English Poems*, Indianapolis, 1966.

Sweet ASR H. Sweet, *Anglo-Saxon Reader*, Oxford, all editions.

Sweet/Onions H. Sweet, *Anglo-Saxon Reader*, revised by C. T. Onions, Oxford, 1946.

Sweet/Whitelock H. Sweet, *Anglo-Saxon Reader*, revised by D. Whitelock, Oxford, 1967.

I

General Account

Only about 30,000 lines of Old English poetry survive; many of the poems which do are fragmentary, and we know the poets and places and dates of composition of almost none of them. Most of the extant verse is known from manuscripts written in Wessex at the end of the tenth century, though in many cases the poems must have been composed long before in other parts of the country, and much of the copying is demonstrably more or less inaccurate. No major works and few minor ones survive in more than one copy, so that the correction of errors and the reconstruction of the originals is extremely difficult and often quite impossible. The selection of what has survived has depended entirely on the chances which have caused this manuscript rather than that to escape fire and the other hazards of time. Yet despite all these disadvantages we still possess a body of poetry which contains a quantity of work of the highest standard and whose variety is astonishing. Even within the great preponderance of Christian poetry many types are represented, including more or less close translations of parts of the Bible, saints' lives, homilies, prayers and allegories; there are also secular poems dealing with battles and other contemporary events, heroic stories from the past, riddles, charms, proverbs, monologues of a personal nature, and, most famous of all, the great epic *Beowulf*, heroic in manner and matter, yet firmly based in the Christian ethos of the period.

Old English poetry had its origins many centuries before among the Germanic peoples on the continent from whom the Anglo-Saxons were descended, as is made clear by the rather similar types of alliterative verse found among other Germanic peoples, for example in Iceland. We can deduce very little in detail about this ancient Germanic poetry. Tacitus tells us of the celebration of their gods in ancient songs, which he describes as their only form of historical record,* and he also states that they sing in praise of Hercules on their way to battle, and that they have another kind of song for inspiring warlike courage.† The first type referred to is probably the direct ancestor of such works as the Icelandic mythical and heroic lays and such Old English poems as *Waldere* (which survives only in two small fragments) and the battle poems. Doubtless from lays of this type the *Beowulf* poet learnt of the historical Scandinavian events which are the setting for his story. It is well-known that even after the conversion English monks still knew and enjoyed the old heroic stories, for in a famous letter Alcuin rebuked them with the question: 'What has Ingeld to do with Christ?' (Ingeld was a famous Germanic hero.) One can only guess that these lays were simple in structure, dealing only with one story, hero or battle at a time. There were probably also collections of proverbial wisdom, ancestors of parts of such works as the Icelandic *Hávamál* and the Old English *Gnomic Verses*, and presumably there were verses of a lighter nature.

Apart from something of the form and subject matter of the Germanic songs, the Anglo-Saxons also inherited much of the ethos of the Germanic society as described by Tacitus, as is seen in *Beowulf, The Wanderer, The Battle of Maldon* and the entry in *The Anglo-Saxon Chronicle* under the year 755.‡ But very rapidly after the conversion the Anglo-Saxons adopted with great thoroughness the culture of the Christianity of the time, which had itself extensively absorbed the culture of classical Rome, and therefore we find in Anglo-Saxon literature almost no trace of a primitive, barbarian and heathen past. *Beowulf* is permeated with Christianity, the *Riddles* are no primitive diversion but imitations of a medieval Latin exercise, and if ever the personal elegiac lyric had an independent Germanic existence it had become thoroughly

---

* Tacitus, *Germania*, II.   † Ibid, III.
‡ G. N. Garmonsway, *The Anglo-Saxon Chronicle Translated with an Introduction*, Everyman's Library, 1953, pp. 46, 48.

converted for Christian purposes in *The Wanderer* and *The Seafarer*.

The earliest Old English poem which can be dated with any accuracy is *Cædmon's Hymn*, composed between 657 and 680; the latest is *Durham*, datable between 1104–9. Apart from the *Paris Psalter*, which consists of more than 5000 lines of translations from the Psalms, and the *Metres of Boethius*, which is probably King Alfred's own translation of the verses in *De Consolatione Philosophiae*, the majority of extant Old English verse survives in four great manuscripts, the Exeter Book, the Vercelli Book, the Junius Manuscript in the Bodleian Library, and the manuscript containing *Beowulf* and *Judith* in the British Museum. Junius and Vercelli are collections of Christian material, the Exeter Book, though predominantly religious, is more heterogeneous. The only poets whose names we know are Cædmon, King Alfred, Aldhelm, of whose Old English verse nothing survives, Bede, whose 5-line poem *Bede's Death Song* must have been written in 735, and one Cynewulf, whose practice it was to end his poems with a coda in which his name was spelt out in the letters of the Runic Alphabet, and about whom nothing else is known except that he was probably a Mercian of the eighth or ninth century.

2

Old English Verse

The Old English verse that survives is remarkably homogeneous in form so that, although we have no contemporary account of the 'rules', they can be deduced with some certainty. The vast majority of lines fit the following description.

Every line is divided into two half-lines containing a minimum of four syllables. Two syllables in each half-line carry a main stress, and at least one of the main stresses in the first half-line must begin with the same consonant sound as the first main stress in the second half-line. For this purpose lack of consonant counts as a consonant sound, so that two words beginning with a vowel sound can alliterate even if the vowel sound is not the same, e.g. *Battle of Maldon* l. 5, *Offan* alliterates with *ærest*. The second stressed syllable of the second half-line should not enter into the alliterative scheme except in a few cases of 'crossed' alliteration, i.e. when the first stressed syllables of the two half-lines alliterate with each other and the second stressed syllables also do, or in cases of 'transverse' alliteration, when the first stress of the first half-line alliterates with the second of the second half-line and *vice versa*. Long ago E. Sievers demonstrated that the patterns of stresses that appear in the half-line can be reduced to five basic types, though extra syllables and other factors give variety and complexity to each of the five types. They may be exemplified as follows:

A Strong weak strong weak: *fírum fóldu* Cædmon's Hymn 9.
B Weak strong weak strong: *on éad, on ǽht* Ruin 36.
C Weak strong strong weak: *on lýft lǽdan* Dream of Rood 5.

D Strong strong weak weak: *béorn blándenfeax*

Battle of Brunanburh 45.

E Strong weak weak strong: *féasceaftig férð* Seafarer 26.

The stressed syllables contain a long vowel or end in a consonant, or if not an extra syllable must follow them, which is called 'resolution'; however there is not always resolution in the second half of A and C types:

A with resolution in first half: *Métodes méowlan* Judith 261.
C without resolution in second half: *his góldgífan* Judith 279.

Syllables extra to the basic pattern may be added in quite large numbers, but they are generally absorbed just before or after the first stress:

B *and tō pǣre hílde stóp* Battle of Maldon 8.

There are also some lines in which there appears to be only one word which can reasonably carry a main stress, such as *mid pā nōpe* Whale 28, *pe pone wiggend* Judith 252, *for pǣm worde* Dream of Rood 111, *in pā ēcan* Seafarer 120, *of langope* Wife's Lament 53.

Recently Professor Pope, while not disputing the general truth of Sievers's theory, has produced a fundamentally different view of Old English versification which has received wide though not universal acceptance.* He argues that the verse was rhythmically regular rather than metrically. There is evidence that in some if not all cases the performance of the poems was accompanied by the harp, which makes it improbable that the verse did not have a regular rhythm; indeed many verse forms lend themselves to regular rhythm in speech even if the poet did not consciously intend it, as for example blank verse. Professor Pope shows that the Old English verses can be made to sound very satisfying if spoken rhythmically in such a way that the timing of the words in the normal verses can be written down according to a musical system of notes and rests, with two bars of two beats each to the half-line. When this is worked out in detail a very large number of Sievers's main stresses prove to fall where one would expect them,

* J. C. Pope, *The Rhythm of Beowulf*, Yale, 1942, revised 1966.

on the first beats of the bars. Such a system can readily accommodate all the variants discussed above and more, whereas theories based more closely on the metrical views of Sievers leave many lines which can only be justified by recourse to a rather improbable complexity.

The discussion so far has referred to the majority of OE half-lines, which may be called 'normal'. There is also a substantial number of much longer lines, usually called 'hypermetric'. Detailed analysis* shows that they were twice the normal length and had as their basis four stresses to the half-line. Such lines tend to slow up the movement of the verse, and when skilfully used can add emphasis in appropriate passages, as in *The Dream of the Rood* ll. 8–10, 59–69, etc., and *The Wanderer* ll. 112–15. Often however they seem merely to be used to give some variety, as in the groups in *Judith*. They almost always appear in groups.

To make the foregoing more clear it is necessary to give some account of the Old English stress system. Within a sentence words which have greater importance for the sense will naturally be spoken with greater emphasis. Therefore, as one would expect, in general nouns, adjectives and most adverbs carry the main stresses, followed in priority by verbs other than auxiliaries; but other parts of speech, such as pronouns, auxiliary verbs and conjunctions, can carry the stress if the sense is such that they would naturally be emphasised.

In Germanic the stress in each word had come to fall on the first syllable, and this remained generally true in Old English. But prefixes on verbs were usually unstressed in OE, as *ārīsan*, 'arise', and the prefixes *ge-* and *be-* were never stressed on any part of speech. In compound words, such as many Proper Names, the second element bore a somewhat weaker stress, e.g. *hílderínc*, *Býrhtnōþ*. This secondary stress could carry a main stress in the verse, but not always, as *góldgífan*, but *féasceaftig férð*. As this shows, one of the many sources of possible variety within the half-line was the presence of an additional but secondary stress.

The alliterative poetry was of course originally oral, composed

* J. C. Pope, op. cit., pp. 99–158.

impromptu by skilled poets called *scopas*, who used well-known material and a highly conventional and formulaic verse form and diction. Literary composition must have begun some years after the conversion of England, though even then the poets must have had oral performance very much in mind. The formulas of the oral period remained useful, and one frequently meets the same half-line in different poems, and sometimes even in the same poem. It must be admitted that at worst the excessive use of well-known formulas can give a rather stilted effect, as perhaps in *The Battle of Brunanburh*, which is a very conventional piece of writing.

The demands of alliteration were met by using large numbers of synonyms for some words, which sometimes took the form of special poetic words such as *hæleþ*, 'warrior', sometimes of specially formed compounds such as *gūþfremmend*, 'war-doer' = 'warrior', sometimes by more extended periphrastic expressions such as *hæleða hlēo*, 'the protector of heroes' = 'the chief', sometimes by metaphorical expressions called 'kennings' such as *hwæles ēþel*, 'the whale's land' = 'the sea'. Attractive though these last are, they are not very original for the most part, and one often meets with the same ones. The demands of the verse form often made it necessary for the poet to repeat himself by referring for example to a warrior twice or more in different ways in quick succession. This can be done very effectively as in *Cædmon's Hymn*, where the large number of ways of saying God are skilfully used to refer to different aspects of His nature, though at its worst it can be clumsy and even absurd.*

Towards the end of the period rhyme was increasingly used as an additional ornament, and in a few poems there appears a tendency to relax the rules outlined above. Yet the verse remained substantially the same throughout the 500 years or so involved. Alliterative verse, though in a modified form, continued to be written and probably composed orally until the fifteenth century. The modifications were the result of adaptation to the changing

* For a valuable account of the diction see H. C. Wyld, 'Diction and Imagery in Anglo-Saxon Poetry', *Essays and Studies*, XL, 1925.

nature of the language. With the decline of the inflectional endings late in the Old English period, word order became fixed in a form not very different from that of the present day, and more auxiliary verbs and prepositions came to be used. English thus became unsuitable for the rather compressed form of Old English verse, and the verse gradually evolved to longer and more flowing lines to be found at their best in fourteenth-century poems such as *Sir Gawain and the Green Knight* and *Piers Plowman*.

Strangely in all this period only two references to the craft of alliterative verse appear. *Beowulf* ll. 867 ff. reads:

> Hwīlum cyninges þegn,
> guma gilphlæden, gidda gemyndig,
> se ðe ealfela ealdgesegena
> worn gemunde, word ōðer fand
> sōðe gebunden; secg eft ongan
> sīð Bēowulfes snyttrum styrian
> ond on spēd wrecan spel gerāde,
> wordum wrixlan.

'Sometimes the king's thane, a man of many stories, mindful of songs, who knew very many of the ancient tales, found different words truly linked together; he afterwards began to proclaim wisely Beowulf's adventure, and to tell the story skilfully, to vary his words.'

This passage gives a clear picture of the *scop* composing impromptu, varying his terms and alliterating correctly. At the other end of the period the poet of 'Sir Gawain' urges on us the antiquity of the alliterative verse, referring to the 'locking of loyal letters':

> If ȝe wyl lysten þis laye bot on littel quile,
> I schal telle hit astit, as I in toun herde,
> with tonge,

As hit is stad and stoken
In stori stif and stronge,
With lel letteres loken,
In londe so hatz ben longe.

'If you will listen to this lay for just a little while, I shall tell it
quickly as I heard it spoken in town, as it is clearly established
in firm, strong story, linked together with loyal letters, as has
long been done in the land.'

3

This Translation

In the translation I have tried to give the sense of the texts as closely as possible. Having decided not to use prose in the faint hope that a verse translation might capture something of the spirit of the original, I had little doubt that blank verse is the proper medium, free verse being far too informal for poetry in verse of so conventional and orderly a type; I also believe that an attempt to produce verse similar in form to the Old English is doomed to failure as the structure of the language is now fundamentally different.

Some of the stylistic features of Old English verse are unfamiliar and liable to sound absurd in modern English, as with the many compound nouns and adjectives and the frequent use of two or more near-synonyms in apposition. I have tried to keep as close to the original as I could while avoiding absurdity. I am well aware that I have not always been successful. The use of such words as 'patron' for a military leader may seem strange, but the Germanic chief was indeed general, patron, distributor of treasures and friend. Where words have been added to fill out a line or explain a difficulty I have said so in the footnotes, though I have not called attention to minor paraphrasing. Some of the names have been modernised in translation, but I have not done so consistently.

I have used all the most famous short Old English poems. For the rest I have tried to choose in such a way as to exemplify as far as possible the wide range of interests of the poets. I found some passages and one or two entire poems very difficult to turn into blank verse, but I was unwilling on those grounds to exclude important and interesting works, so I have done my best. I have avoided the longer poems and give no selection from *Beowulf*, of which many translations already exist.

The texts of some of the poems are taken directly from printed editions as acknowledged in the Preface. The others are the result of my own consideration of the various editions. The texts as given contain numerous emendations to the manuscript readings, and these are listed on pp. 205–7. Long vowels are marked to help the reader who wishes to try the poems aloud. All punctuation is editorial and must not be regarded as necessarily established.

The Ruin

This is a reflective description of the ruins of some Roman city, most probably Bath. Unfortunately the Exeter Book is damaged at this point, whence the missing sections after l. 11 and at the end. Although there is no clear indication of it in the text, it seems likely that the poem should be considered in the context of the Christian view of history to be found in some medieval Latin poems dealing with the decline of great cities, on which see the discussion of *Durham* below.

BIBLIOGRAPHY

Kershaw
ASPR III
R. F. Leslie, *Three Old English Elegies*, Manchester, 1961

The Ruin

Wrǣtlic is þes wealstān;   wyrde gebrǣcon,
burgstede burston,   brosnað enta geweorc.
Hrōfas sind gehrorene,   hrēorge torras,
hrungeat berofen,   hrīm on līme,
5 scearde scūrbeorge   scorene, gedrorene,
ældo undereotone.   Eorðgrāp hafað
waldendwyrhtan,   forweorone, geleorene,
heard gripe hrūsan,   oþ hund cnēa
werþēoda gewitan.   Oft þæs wāg gebād,
10 rǣghār and rēadfāh,   rīce æfter ōþrum,
ofstonden under stormum;   stēap gēap gedrēas.

. . . .

Mōd monade,   myne swiftne gebrægd;
hwætrēd in hringas,   hygerōf gebond
20 weallwalan wīrum   wundrum tōgædre.
Beorht wǣron burgrǣced,   burnsele monige,
hēah horngestrēon,   heroswēg micel,
meodoheall monig   mondrēama full,
oþþæt þæt onwende   wyrd sēo swīþe.
25 Crungon walo wīde,   cwōman wōldagas,
swylt eall fornōm   secgrōfra wera;
wurdon hyra wīgsteal   wēstenstaþolas,
brosnade burgsteall.   Bētend crungon,
hergas tō hrūsan.   Forþon þās hofu drēorgiað
30 and þæs tēaforgēapa   tigelum scēadeð

---

2. *enta geweorc*. 'The works of giants' appear several times on OE poetry referring to large ancient buildings, usually Roman survivals. See *Gnomic Verses* l. 2, and also note to *Wanderer* l. 87 where giants may be literally intended.

12–17. Some words and letters are legible in the MS, but not enough to make interpretation possible.

18. *monade* and *myne* proposed by Leslie, only *mo-* and *-yne* being legible.

The Ruin

Splendid this rampart is, though fate destroyed it,
The city buildings fell apart, the works
Of giants crumble. Tumbled are the towers,
Ruined the roofs, and broken the barred gate,
Frost in the plaster, all the ceilings gape,
Torn and collapsed and eaten up by age.
And grit holds in its grip, the hard embrace
Of earth, the dead departed master-builders,
Until a hundred generations now
Of people have passed by. Often this wall
Stained red and grey with lichen has stood by
Surviving storms while kingdoms rose and fell.
And now the high curved wall itself has fallen.

. . . .

The heart inspired, incited to swift action.
Resolute masons, skilled in rounded building
Wondrously linked the framework with iron bonds.
The public halls were bright, with lofty gables,
Bath-houses many; great the cheerful noise,
And many mead-halls filled with human pleasures.
Till mighty fate brought change upon it all.
Slaughter was widespread, pestilence was rife,
And death took all those valiant men away.
The martial halls became deserted places,
The city crumbled, its repairers fell,
Its armies to the earth. And so these halls
Are empty, and this red curved roof now sheds

hrōstbēages hrōf.　　Hryre wong gecrong
　　gebrocen tō beorgum　　þǣr iū beorn monig
　　glædmōd and goldbeorht　　gleoma gefrætwed,
　　wlonc and wīngāl　　wīghyrstum scān,
35　seah on sinc, on sylfor,　　on searogimmas,
　　on ēad, on æht,　　on eorcanstān,
　　on þās beorhtan burg　　brādan rīces.
　　Stānhofu stōdan,　　strēam hāte wearp
　　wīdan wylme;　　weal eall befeng
40　beorhtan bōsme　　þǣr þā baþu wǣron,
　　hāt on hreþre;　　þæt wæs hyðelic.
　　Lēton þonne gēotan　　. . . . .
　　ofer hārne stān　　hāte strēamas
　　under . . . .　　. . . . .
45　oþþæt hringmere.　　Hāte . . . . . .
　　. . . . .　　þǣr þā baþu wǣron.
　　. . . . .

42–end. From this point most of the poem is illegible and the translation
is a guess. From l. 45 on no sense can be deduced.

Its tiles, decay has brought it to the ground,
Smashed it to piles of rubble, where long since
A host of heroes, glorious, gold-adorned,
Gleaming in splendour, proud and flushed with wine,
Shone in their armour, gazed on gems and treasure,
On silver, riches, wealth and jewellery,
On this bright city with its wide domains.
Stone buildings stood, and the hot stream cast forth
Wide sprays of water, which a wall enclosed
In its bright compass, where convenient
Stood hot baths ready for them at the centre.
Hot streams poured forth over the clear grey stone,
To the round pool and down into the baths.

. . . .

Durham

This, the latest datable OE poem, was written between 1104 and 1109. Though it appears a simple piece, it has in fact a long and learned history. The *encomium urbis* was an established type even in classical Greece, and ancient writers on Poetic laid down in great detail what should be said about a city and how and in what order. Many early medieval examples in Latin are extant, including one on York by Alcuin. A by-product of this type, resulting from the influence of Christianity, was one in which the former glories of a city were contrasted with its present state of decline or destruction, among which Alcuin wrote one on Lindisfarne. It may be that *The Ruin* owes something to this category. *Durham* is a very brief example, yet everything in it has strong echoes in one or other of the others extant.

BIBLIOGRAPHY

ASPR VI
M. Schlauch, 'An Old English *Encomium Urbis*', *Journal of English and Germanic Philology*, XL, 1941

Durham

Is ðēos burch brēome   geond Breotenrīce,
stēppa gestaðolad,   stānas ymbūtan
wundrum gewæxen.   Weor ymbeornad
ēa ȳðum stronge,   and ðēr inne wunað
5 feola fisca kyn   on flōda gemonge.
And ðǣr gewexen is   wudafæstern micel;
wuniad in ðēm wȳcum   wilda dēor monige,
in dēope dalum   dēora ungerīm.
Is in ðēre byri ēac   bearnum gecȳðed
10 ðe ārfesta   ēadig Cūdberch
and ðes clēne   cyninges hēafud,
Ōsuualdes, Engle lēo,   and Aidan biscop,
Ēadberch and Ēadfrið,   æðele gefēres.
Is ðēr inne midd heom   Æðelwold biscop
15 and brēoma bōcera Bēda,   and Boisil abbot,
ðe clēne Cūdberte   on gecheðe
lērde lustum,   and hē his lāra wel genom.
Eardiæð æt ðēm ēadige   in in ðēm minstre
unārīmeda   reliquia,
20 ðǣr monia wundrum gewurðað,   ðes ðe writ seggeð,
midd ðene Drihnes wer   dōmes bīdeð.

Durham

This city is renowned throughout all Britain,
Set on steep slopes and marvellously built
With rocks all round. A strongly running river
Flows past enclosed by weirs, and therein dwell
All kinds of fishes in the seething waters.
And there a splendid forest has grown up;
Many wild animals live in those places,
And countless beasts inhabit the deep dales.
Within that town, as is well-known to men,
There lies the blessed saint, the pious Cuthbert.
There also lies the head of chaste King Oswald,
England's protector, as does Bishop Aidan,
And the two noble lords, Eadberch and Eadfrith.
Therein with them are Bishop Athelwold,
The famous scholar Bede and Abbot Boisil
Who taught pure Cuthbert in his youthful days
Gladly, and he received his teaching well.
Inside the minster by the blessed saint
Are relics numberless; there multitudes
Of miracles take place, as books make known,
While there God's servant lies and waits for Judgment

The Fight at Finnsburh

The manuscript of this fragment was found by George Hickes in Lambeth Palace Library, and he printed the text in 1705. Unfortunately his standard of transcription was not very high, as is known from other examples of his work, and the manuscript has never since been found. It seems that this fragment is part of a poem which told the whole story of a feud between a branch of the Danes and the Frisians. The only other information about the story comes from *Beowulf* ll. 1063-1159, but this account too is incomplete. The *scop* is entertaining the Danish court and their guests, Beowulf and his party, with a story in the hall, and the poet of *Beowulf* only gives the part of the story which is relevant to the major events in his poem, in the confidence that the rest of the tale is well known. The part used is not the same as that in the fragment, and much recent scholarship has been devoted to discussion of the relationship between the two accounts. The best discussion is to be found in R. W. Chambers, *Beowulf, An Introduction*, 3rd edition with a supplement by C. L. Wrenn, Cambridge, 1959, pp. 245-90. The story appears to go something like this: There had been a war between the Danes and Frisians, which was settled, and as often happened the opposing parties compounded their peace agreement by a marriage, in this case between Finn, king of the Frisians, and Hildeburh, sister of Hnæf, who either was or became a king of the Half-Danes. Many years later, when Finn and Hildeburh had a son old enough to fight, a Danish party under Hnæf visited Finn at a place called Finnsburh whose location is unknown. There were Jutes with one side or the other, possibly even with both. For some reason fighting broke out, and Hnæf's men were attacked by night in a hall (the fragment begins here). The battle was long and bloody, and after many including Finn's son and Hnæf had been killed, stalemate was

34

reached (the *Beowulf* section begins). Finn came to terms with Hengest, who now led the Danish party, and the Danes remained with Finn during the ensuing winter. But with the coming of spring desire for vengeance became too strong for the Danes, Finn was killed, and Hengest's party returned home taking Hildeburh with them. The part played by the Jutes in all this is very unclear though certainly important, as the *Beowulf* account starts with the statement that 'Hildeburh had no need to praise the good faith of the Jutes; guiltless she was deprived of her loved ones at the battle-play, of son and brother'. It must be stressed that all the earlier part of the summary here offered is 'reasonable' deduction based on no shred of evidence.

The fragment is a vivid and striking piece. It appears to begin with two carefully balanced speeches, though only the last word and a half of the first survive, '*-nas byrnað*', answered by '*hornas ne byrnað*' l. 4. Carrion beasts appear ll. 5–6, a conventional description of bravery and loyal repayment of a lord's generosity is given in ll. 37–40, and the method of portraying battle largely by speeches is employed here as in *The Battle of Maldon*. That one warrior should urge another not to risk his life in the first onslaught, ll. 18–21, is perhaps surprising (compare *Gnomic Verses* ll. 15–16) but the intention is presumably to emphasise the heroism of Garulf by his rejection of this unheroic advice.

BIBLIOGRAPHY

ASPR VI

Fr. Klaeber, *Beowulf and the Fight at Finnsburg*, New York, 1922, pp. 231–53

   . . . .   hornas byrnað.'
Hnæf hlēoþrode ðā   heaþogeong cyning:
'Ne ðis ne dagað ēastan,   ne hēr draca ne flēogeð,
ne hēr ðisse healle   hornas ne byrnað;
5   ac hēr forþ berað,   fugelas singað,
gylleð grǣghama,   gūðwudu hlynneð,
scyld scefte oncwyð.   Nū scȳneð þes mōna
waðol under wolcnum;   nū ārīsað wēadǣda,
ðe ðisne folces nīð   fremman willað.
10   Ac onwacnigeað nū,   wīgend mīne,
habbað ēowre linda,   hicgeaþ on ellen,
winnað on orde,   wesað on mōde!'
    Ðā ārās mænig goldhladen ðegn,   gyrde hine his swurde;
ðā tō dura ēodon   drihtlice cempan,
15   Sigeferð and Ēaha,   hyra sword getugon,
and æt ōþrum durum   Ordlāf and Gūþlāf,
and Hengest sylf,   hwearf him on lāste.
    Ðā gȳt Gārulfe   Gūðere stȳrde,
ðæt hē swā frēolic feorh   forman sīþe
20   tō ðǣre healle durum   hyrsta ne bǣre,
nū hyt nīþa heard   ānyman wolde;
ac hē frægn ofer eal   undearninga,
dēormōd hæleþ,   hwā ðā duru hēolde.
'Sigeferþ is mīn nama (cweþ hē),   ic eom Secgena lēod,
25   wreccea wīde cūð;   fæla ic wēana gebād,
heordra hilda;   ðē is gȳt hēr witod,
swæþer ðū sylf tō mē   sēcean wylle.'
    Ðā wæs on healle   wælslihta gehlyn,
sceolde cellod bord   cēnum on handa,
30   bānhelm berstan,   buruhðelu dynede,

---

29. *cellod* Hickes *Celæs.* This word is otherwise unknown and many
editors substitute *cellod* from *Battle of Maldon* l. 283; but *cellod* only occurs
there and is equally mysterious.
30. 'thundered' added in translation.

The Fight at Finnsburh

... 'Or are the gables burning on this hall?'
Hnæf answered him, the young and warlike king:
'No eastern dawn is this, no dragon flying,
Nor are the gables burning on this hall.
But now starts war; the carrion-birds shall sing,
The grey-cloaked wolf shall yell, the spear resound,
Shield answer shaft. Now shines the wandering moon
Behind the clouds. Now rise up deeds of woe
Which will bring suffering upon this people.
But wake yourselves my warriors now, and take
Your shields, and set your minds on gallant deeds,
Fight at the front, and be of noble heart'.
Then many a treasure-laden thane arose
And put his sword on; two brave champions
Eaha and Sigeferth went to the door
And drew their swords, while at the other door
Ordlaf and Guthlaf stood, and in their track
Hengest himself advanced. Still Guthere
Urged Garulf not to risk in the first rush
Upon the doors his arms and noble life,
Now war-hard warriors would deprive him of it;
But he asked loudly and without concealment,
The worthy hero, who there held the doors.
'Sigeferth is my name, a Secgan prince,'
He answered, 'An adventurer well-known.
I have seen many fierce and grievous battles.
And fate already has laid down for you
One of two outcomes of our meeting here.'
Then was the sound of slaughter in the hall.
Curved shields in bold men's hands, and helmets hard
Burst, and the hall-floor thundered and resounded,

oð æt ðære gūðe   Gārulf gecrang
ealra ærest   eorðbūendra,
Gūðlāfes sunu,   ymbe hyne gōdra fæla,
hwearflīcra hræw.   Hræfen wandrode
35 sweart and sealobrūn.   Swurdlēoma stōd,
swylce eal Finnsburuh   fȳrenu wære.
Ne gefrægn ic næfre wurþlīcor   æt wera hilde
sixtig sigebeorna   sēl gebæran,
ne nēfre swānas hwītne medo   sēl forgyldan,
40 ðonne Hnæfe guldan   his hægstealdas.
Hig fuhton fīf dagas,   swā hyra nān ne fēol,
drihtgesīða,   ac hig ðā duru hēoldon.
Ðā gewāt him wund hæleð   on wæg gangan,
sæde þæt his byrne   ābrocen wære,
45 heresceorp unhrōr,   and ēac wæs his helm ðȳrel.
Ðā hine sōna frægn   folces hyrde,
hū ðā wīgend hyra   wunda genæson,
oððe hwæþer ðæra hyssa   . . . .

47. *hyra* should probably begin the second half-line, see Pope, *Rhythm of Beowulf*, p. 83.

Till in the battle Garulf died, the son
Of Guthlaf perished first of all that host,
And round him many noble heroes fell,
The corpses of the brave. The raven circled
Swarthy and sallow. Swords flashed constantly
As if all Finnsborough were set on fire.
I've never heard of sixty warriors
Behaving better in a mortal fight,
Or for sweet mead a finer recompense
Than the young warriors repaid to Hnæf.
The comrades fought for five full days, and none
Of them was slain, but they held fast the doors.
A wounded hero then went on his way,
Said that his corslet now was broken through,
His armour useless and his helmet pierced.
The general at once enquired of him
How well the warriors endured their wounds,
Or whether any of the young retainers . . .

The Battle of Brunanburh

The Battle of Brunanburh took place in 937 between a combined
army of Norsemen from Ireland under Anlaf and Scots under
Constantine and another combined army of Mercians and West
Saxons under the West Saxon brothers Æthelstan and Eadmund.
No more can be decided about the site of the battle than the poem
tells us, that it took place outside Wessex and outside the kingdom
of Constantine and probably not very far from the sea, the sea in
question being most likely the Irish Sea, as the Norse survivors
returned to Dublin. Identification of the place-names Brunanburh
and Dingesmere has proved impossible.

In view of the late date of the poem, it is, though vivid,
surprisingly conventional, with its description of the passage of
a day, ll. 12–17, its references to carrion beasts, ll. 60–5, and the
two characteristically grim examples of litotes, ll. 39–40 and 44–9,
the latter followed by the long list of varied expressions for battle.

BIBLIOGRAPHY

A. Campbell, *The Battle of Brunanburh*, London, 1938
The text here used is that of Campbell with the long vowels
marked.

41

Æþelstān cyning,   eorla dryhten,
beorna bēahgifa,   and his brōþor ēac,
Ēadmund æþeling,   ealdorlangne tīr
geslōgon æt sæcce   sweorda ecgum
5 ymbe Brunanburh;   bordweal clufan,
hēowan heaþolinde   hamora lāfan
afaran Ēadweardes;   swā him geæþele wæs
from cnēomǣgum,   þæt hī æt campe oft
wiþ lāþra gehwæne   land ealgodon,
10 hord and hāmas.   Hettend crungun,
Sceotta leōda   and scipflotan
fǣge fēollan.   Feld dunnade
secga swāte,   siðþan sunne up
on morgentīd,   mǣre tungol,
15 glād ofer grundas,   Godes condel beorht,
ēces Drihtnes,   oð sīo æþele gesceaft
sāh tō setle.   Þǣr læg secg mænig
gārum āgēted,   guma norþerna
ofer scild scoten,   swilce Scittisc ēac
20 wērig, wīges sæd.   Wesseaxe forð
ondlongne dæg   ēorodcistum
on lāst legdun   lāþum þēodum,
hēowan hereflēman   hindan þearle
mēcum mylenscearpan.   Myrce ne wyrndon
25 heardes hondplegan   hæleþa nānum
þæra þe mid Anlāfe   ofer ēargebland
on lides bōsme   land gesōhtun
fǣge to gefeohte.   Fīfe lǣgun
on þām campstede   cyningas giunge
30 sweordum āswefede,   swilce seofene ēac
eorlas Anlāfes,   unrīm heriges,
flotena and Sceotta.   Þǣr geflēmed wearð
Norðmanna bregu,   nēde gebēded
tō lides stefne   lītle weorode;

The Battle of Brunanburh

King Athelstan, the lord of warriors,
Patron of heroes, and his brother too,
Prince Edmund, won themselves eternal glory
In battle with the edges of their swords
Round Brunanburh; they broke the wall of shields,
The sons of Edward with their well-forged swords
Slashed at the linden-shields; such was their nature
From boyhood that in battle they had often
Fought for their land, its treasures and its homes,
Against all enemies. Their foes fell dead,
The Scottish soldiers and the pirate host
Were doomed to perish; and with blood of men
The field was darkened from the time the sun
Rose at the break of day, the glorious star,
God the eternal Lord's bright candle passed
Across the land, until this noble creature
Sank to its resting-place. There many men
Lay slain by spears, and northern warriors
Shot down despite their shields, and Scotsmen too,
Weary, with battle sated. The West Saxons
Throughout the whole long passing of the day
Pressed on in troops behind the hostile people,
Hewed fiercely from the rear the fleeing host
With well-ground swords. The Mercians refused
Hard battle-play to none among the fighters
Who came with Anlaf over rolling seas,
Bringing invasion to this land by ship,
Destined to die in battle. Five young kings
Lay dead upon the battlefield, by swords
Sent to their final sleep; and likewise seven
Of Anlaf's earls, and countless of his host,
Both Scots and seamen. There the Norsemen's chief
Was put to flight, and driven by dire need
With a small retinue to seek his ship.

35 créad cnear on flot,   cyning út gewát
on fealene flód,   feorh generede.

Swilce þær éac se fróda   mid fléame cóm
on his cýþþe norð,   Costontínus,
hár hildering;   hréman ne þorfte
40 mecga gemánan: hé wæs his mæga sceard,
fréonda befylled   on folcstede,
beslagen æt sæcce,   and his sunu forlét
on wælstówe   wundun forgrunden,
giungne æt gúðe.   Gelpan ne þorfte
45 beorn blandenfeax   bilgeslehtes,
eald inwidda,   ne Anláf þý má;
mid heora hereláfum   hlehhan ne þorftun,
þæt héo beaduweorca   beteran wurdun
on campstede,   cumbolgehnástes,
50 gármittinge,   gumena gemótes,
wæpengewrixles,   þæs hí on wælfelda
wiþ Éadweardes   afaran plegodan.

Gewitan him þá Norþmen   nægledcnearrum,
dréorig daraða láf,   on Dingesmere,
55 ofer déop wæter   Difelin sécan,
eft Íra land,   æwiscmóde.

Swilce þá gebróþer   bégen ætsamne,
cyning and æþeling,   cýþþe sóhton,
Wesseaxena land,   wíges hrémge.
60 Létan him behindan   hræ bryttian
saluwigpádan,   þone sweartan hræfn,
hyrnednebban,   and þane hasupádan,
earn æftan hwít,   æses brúcan
grædigne gúðhafoc   and þæt græge déor,
65 wulf on wealde.   Ne wearð wæl máre
on þis éiglande   æfre gíeta
folces gefylled   beforan þissum
sweordes ecgum,   þæs þe ús secgað béc,
ealde úðwitan,   siþþan éastan hider
70 Engle and Seaxe   up becóman,

44

The ship pressed out to sea, the king departed
Onto the yellow flood and saved his life.
Likewise the wise old Constantinus came,
The veteran, to his northern native land
By flight; he had no reason to exult
In that encounter; for he lost there friends
And was deprived of kinsmen in the strife
Upon that battlefield, and left his son
Destroyed by wounds on that grim place of slaughter,
The young man in the fight. The grey-haired man
Had little cause to boast about that battle,
The sly old soldier, any more than Anlaf;
They could not with their remnant laugh and claim
That they were better in their warlike deeds
When banners met upon the battlefield,
Spears clashed and heroes greeted one another,
Weapons contended, when they played at war
With Edward's sons upon the place of carnage.
The Norsemen left them in their well-nailed ships,
The sad survivors of the darts, on Dingsmere
Over the deep sea back they went to Dublin,
To Ireland they returned with shameful hearts.
The brothers also both went home together,
The king and prince returned to their own country,
The land of Wessex, triumphing in war.
They left behind them corpses for the dark
Black-coated raven, horny-beaked to enjoy,
And for the eagle, white-backed and dun-coated,
The greedy war-hawk, and that grey wild beast
The forest wolf. Nor has there on this island
Been ever yet a greater number slain,
Killed by the edges of the sword before
This time, as books make known to us, and old
And learned scholars, after hither came
The Angles and the Saxons from the east,

ofer brād brimu   Brytene sōhtan,
wlance wīgsmiþas,   Wēalas ofercōman,
eorlas ārhwate,   eard begēatan.

Over the broad sea sought the land of Britain,
Proud warmakers, victorious warriors,
Conquered the Welsh, and so obtained this land.

The Battle of Maldon

The battle took place in 991 on the mainland opposite the island of Northey not far from Maldon in Essex. The causeway linking the island and the mainland, though subsequently improved, was not very different from its present form, dry at low tide, covered at high.

Despite the late date of the poem, it is very heroic in character and has many points of similarity to Tacitus's description of the conduct of the Germanic warrior, as well as to other Old English works of a heroic nature, notably the *Anglo-Saxon Chronicle* entry for the year 755 and *Beowulf*. The most obvious example is in the system of loyalties; compare ll. 223–4 with the words of the Chronicle entry: 'Ond þā cuǣdon hīe þæt nǣnig mǣg lēofra nǣre þonne hiera hlāford . . .' (And then they said that no kinsman was dearer than their lord . . .).

It has been argued that the battle was lost because of Byrhtnoþ's pride, this view being based on the word *ofermōde*, l. 89. But though *ofermōd* elsewhere means 'pride' it is likely that it could also mean 'over-confidence'. Perhaps the over-confidence here was in the loyalty of his men.

The poem is in many ways very traditional. It is probably a propaganda piece, extolling the ancient standards of conduct and courage while illustrating the contemporary effects of failure in their practice. The reign of Ethelred was noteworthy for constant practice of treachery and cowardice.

BIBLIOGRAPHY

E. D. Laborde, *Byrhtnoth and Maldon*, London, 1936
E. V. Gordon, *The Battle of Maldon*, Methuen's Old English Library, London, 1937
Sweet ASR

ASPR VI

Pope, 7 OE P

J. R. R. Tolkien, 'The Homecoming of Beorhtnoth', *Essays and Studies*, VI, 1953

N. F. Blake, 'The Battle of Maldon', *Neophilologus*, XLIX, 1965

O. D. Macrae-Gibson, *'How Historical is the Battle of Maldon?'*, *Medium Ævum*, XXXIX, 1970

. . . . brocen wurde.
Hēt þā hyssa hwæne   hors forlǣtan,
feor āfȳsan,   and forð gangan,
hicgan tō handum   and tō hige gōdum.
5 Þā þæt Offan mæg   ǣrest onfunde
þæt se eorl nolde   yrhðo geþolian,
hē lēt him þā of handon   lēofne flēogan
hafoc wið þæs holtes,   and tō þǣre hilde stōp.
Be þām man mihte oncnāwan   þæt se cniht nolde
10 wācian æt þām wīge   þā hē tō wǣpnum feng.
Ēac him wolde Ēadrīc   his ealdre gelǣstan,
frēan tō gefeohte;   ongan þā forð beran
gār tō gūþe.   Hē hæfde gōd geþanc
þā hwīle þe hē mid handum   healdan mihte
15 bord and brād swurd;   bēot hē gelǣste
þā hē ætforan his frēan   feohtan sceolde.
     Ðā þǣr Byrhtnōð ongan   beornas trymian,
rād and rǣdde,   rincum tǣhte
hū hī sceoldon standan   and þone stede healdan,
20 and bæd þæt hyra randas   rihte hēoldon
fæste mid folman,   and ne forhtedon nā.
Þā hē hæfde þæt folc   fægere getrymmed,
hē līhte þā mid lēodon   þǣr him lēofost wæs,
þǣr hē his heorðwerod   holdost wiste.
25   Þā stōd on stæðe,   stīðlīce clypode
wīcinga ār,   wordum mǣlde,
se on bēot ābēad   brimlīþendra
ǣrænde tō þām eorle   þǣr hē on ōfre stōd:
'Mē sendon tō þē   sǣmen snelle,
30 hēton ðē secgan   þæt þū mōst sendan raðe
bēagas wið gebeorge,   and ēow betere is
þæt gē þisne gārrǣs   mid gafole forgyldon
þon wē swā hearde   hilde dǣlon.
Ne þurfe wē ūs spillan   gif gē spēdaþ tō þām;

The Battle of Maldon

He ordered then that each young warrior
Should leave his horse and drive it far away,
Advance, and think on arms and noble valour.
Then first did Offa's kinsman understand
That the earl would not suffer indolence,
And made his pet hawk fly out of his hands
Towards the wood, and stepped himself to battle;
Thus could be known that when the young man took
Up arms he would not weaken in the fight.
And Eadrich too resolved to serve his prince,
His lord in battle, and he started forth,
Bearing his spear. His heart remained heroic
As long as he might hold broad sword and shield.
Now that the time had come for him to fight
Before his lord, he duly kept his vow.
Then Byrhtnoth started to arrange his troops,
Rode and advised, and showed the warriors
How they should stand and hold their place, and bade
That they should hold their shields up properly,
Firm in their fists, and should not be afraid.
When he had all his troops correctly placed
He left his horse and joined the army where
His own most dear and loyal hearth-troop stood.
A viking messenger stood on the bank,
Called clearly forth and made his declaration,
Proudly proclaimed the message of the seamen
To Byrhtnoth as he stood upon the shore.
'Bold seamen send me to you, order me
To tell you that you speedily must send
Rings for defence; it would be better for you
To buy off this armed onslaught with your tribute
Than that our hardy men should deal out war.
We need not fight if you can come to terms.

35 wē willað wið þām golde   grið fæstnian.
  Gyf þū þat gerǣdest   þe hēr rīcost eart,
  þæt þū þīne lēoda   lȳsan wille,
  syllan sǣmannum   on hyra sylfra dōm
  feoh wið frēode   and niman frið æt ūs,
40 wē willaþ mid þām sceattum   ūs tō scype gangan,
  on flot fēran   and ēow friþes healdan.'
  Byrhtnōð maþelode,   bord hafenode,
  wand wācne æsc,   wordum mǣlde,
  yrre and ānrǣd   āgeaf him andsware:
45 'Gehȳrst þū, sǣlida,   hwæt þis folc segeð?
  Hī willað ēow tō gafole   gāras syllan,
  ǣttryne ord   and ealde swurd,
  þā heregeatu   þe ēow æt hilde ne dēah.
  Brimmanna boda,   ābēod eft ongēan,
50 sege þīnum lēodum   miccle lāþre spell,
  þæt hēr stynt unforcūð   eorl mid his werode
  þe wile gealgean   ēþel þysne,
  Æþelredes eard,   ealdres mīnes
  folc and foldan.   Feallan sceolon
55 hǣþene æt hilde.   Tō hēanlic mē þinceð
  þæt gē mid ūrum sceattum   tō scype gangon
  unbefohtene   nū gē þus feor hider
  on ūrne eard   in becōmon.
  Ne sceole gē swā sōfte   sinc gegangan;
60 ūs sceal ord and ecg   ǣr gesēman,
  grim gūðplega,   ǣr wē gofol syllon.'
  Hēt þā bord beran,   beornas gangan,
  þæt hī on þām ēasteðe   ealle stōdon.
  Ne mihte þǣr for wætere   werod tō þām ōðrum;
65 þǣr cōm flōwende   flōd æfter ebban,

---

48. *heregeatu* means literally 'war-gear', but it had a technical sense referring to the dues, originally consisting of war equipment, to be repaid to a lord on his tenant's death. See NED under *heriot*. Byrhtnoth's rejoinder is therefore heavily ironical.

We will establish with that gold a truce.
If you who are in charge here will agree
That you are willing to protect your people,
And pay the seamen at their own demand
Money for peace, and take a truce from us,
We with that treasure will embark again,
Go back to sea, and keep the peace with you.'
Byrhtnoth replied, he raised his shield aloft,
Brandished his slender spear, and spoke these words,
Angry and resolute he answered him:
'Do you hear, seaman, what this people says?
They plan to give you nought but spears for tribute,
Poisonous point and edge of tried old sword,
War-tax that will not help you in the fight.
Go, viking herald, answer back again,
Tell to your men a much more hostile tale:
Here stands an earl undaunted with his troop,
One who intends to save this fatherland,
Ethelred's kingdom, and my liege lord's land
And people. It shall be the heathen host
That falls in fight. It seems to me too shameful
That you should take our tribute to your ships
Without a fight, now that you have advanced
So far onto our soil. You shall not win
Treasure so easily; but spear and sword
Must first decide between us, the grim sport
Of war, before we pay our tribute to you.'
He then commanded all his men to take
Their shields and stand along the river bank.
But neither side might there approach the other
For water: the tide rose after the ebb,

lucon lagustrēamas;   tō lang hit him þūhte
hwænne hī tōgædere   gāras bēron.
Hī þǣr Pantan strēam   mid prasse bestōdon,
Ēastseaxena ord   and se æschere;
70 ne mihte hyra ǣnig   ōðrum derian,
būton hwā þurh flānes flyht   fyl genāme.
Se flōd ūt gewāt;   þā flotan stōdon gearowe,
wīcinga fela   wīges georne.
Hēt þā hæleða hlēo   healdan þā bricge
75 wigan wīgheardne,   se wæs hāten Wulfstān,
cāfne mid his cynne,   þæt wæs Cēolan sunu,
þe ðone forman man   mid his francan ofscēat,
þe þǣr baldlīcost   on þā bricge stōp.
Þǣr stōdon mid Wulfstāne   wigan unforhte,
80 Ælfere and Maccus,   mōdige twēgen,
þā noldon æt þām forda   flēam gewyrcan,
ac hī fæstlīce   wið ðā fȳnd weredon
þā hwīle þe hī wæpna   wealdan mōston.
Þā hī þæt ongēaton   and georne gesāwon
85 þæt hī þǣr bricgweardas   bitere fundon,
ongunnon lytegian þā   lāðe gystas,
bǣdon þæt hī upgangan   āgan mōston,
ofer þone ford faran,   fēþan lǣdan.   *over confidence*
Ðā se eorl ongan   for his <u>ofermōde</u>
90 ālȳfan landes tō fela   lāþere ðēode.
Ongan ceallian þā   ofer cald wæter
Byrhtelmes bearn   (beornas gehlyston):
'Nū ēow is gerȳmed,   gāð ricene tō ūs,
guman tō gūþe.   God āna wāt
95 hwā þǣre wælstōwe   wealdan mōte.'
    Wōdon þa wælwulfas,   for wætere ne murnon,
wīcinga werod   west ofer Pantan,
ofer scīr wæter   scyldas wēgon,

70-1 Literally: 'nor might any of them harm another unless one should receive death through an arrow's flight.'

The streaming waters joined. It seemed too long
Before they could engage in deadly combat.
And so they lined the waters of the Pante,
The troops of Essex and the viking army
In fine array; but none could give a wound,
Unless an arrow's flight should take its toll.
The tide receded, seamen ready stood,
A host of vikings eager to start battle.
The earl then called a hardened warrior
To guard the causeway, Wulfstan, Ceola's son,
Of a brave family a kinsman brave,
And with his spear he shot the foremost man
That boldly stepped upon the causeway there.
There stood with Wulfstan dauntless warriors,
Maccus and Alfere, two doughty men,
Who would not at that ford resort to flight,
But stoutly fought against the enemy
As long as they survived to wield their weapons.
When they perceived and clearly understood
That fierce defenders met them on the causeway,
Then did the hateful strangers turn to guile,
Asked that safe passage might be granted them
So that their infantry could cross the ford.
Then in his over-confidence the earl
Yielded to the invaders too much land.
The soldiers stood and listened as the son
Of Byrhtelm called across the cold clear water:
'Now room is made for you; come quickly to us,
Men to the war; and God alone can tell
Who at the end may hold this battlefield.'
The wolves of war advanced, the viking troop,
Unmoved by water, westward over Pante,
Over the gleaming water bore their shields.

lidmen tō lande   linde bǣron.
100 Þǣr ongēan gramum   gearowe stōdon
Byrhtnōð mid beornum;   hē mid bordum hēt
wyrcan þone wīhagan,   and þæt werod healdan
fæste wið fēondum.   Þā wæs feohte nēh,
tīr æt getohte.   Wæs sēo tīd cumen
105 þæt þǣr fǣge men   feallan sceoldon.
Þǣr wearð hrēam āhafen;   hremmas wundon,
earn ǣses georn;   wæs on eorþan cyrm.
Hī lēton þā of folman   fēolhearde speru,
grimme gegrundene   gāras flēogan.
110 Bogan wǣron bysige,   bord ord onfeng,
biter wæs se beadurǣs,   beornas fēollon
on gehwæðere hand,   hyssas lāgon.
Wund wearð Wulfmǣr,   wælrǣste gecēas
Byrhtnōðes mǣg;   hē mid billum wearð,
115 his swustersunu,   swīðe forhēawen.
Þǣr wearð wīcingum   wiþerlēan āgyfen.
Gehȳrde ic þæt Ēadweard   ānne slōge
swīðe mid his swurde,   swenges ne wyrnde,
þæt him æt fōtum fēoll   fǣge cempa;
120 þæs him his ðēoden   þanc gesǣde,
þām būrþēne,   þā hē byre hæfde.
Swā stemnetton   stīðhicgende
hysas æt hilde,   hogodon georne
hwā þǣr mid orde   ǣrost mihte
125 on fǣgean men   feorh gewinnan,
wigan mid wǣpnum;   wæl fēol on eorðan.
Stōdon stædefæste,   stihte hī Byrhtnōð,
bæd þæt hyssa gehwylc   hogode tō wīge,
þe on Denon wolde   dōm gefeohtan.

107. 'Fateful' added in translation.
126. *wigan mid wæpnum* omitted in translation.

The seamen brought their linden-shields to land.
There Byrhtnoth and his warriors stood ready
To meet their enemies. He told his troops
To make a shield-wall and to hold it fast
Against their foes. So battle with its glory
Drew near. The time had come for fated men
To perish in that place. A cry went up.
The ravens wheeled above, the fateful eagle
Keen for his carrion. On earth was uproar.
They let the file-hard spears fly from their fists,
Grimly-ground darts; and bows were busy too,
Shield received spear-point; savage was the onslaught.
Fighters fell dead, young men on either side.
Wulfmar was wounded, Byrhtnoth's sister's son
Chose death in battle, he was utterly
Cut down by swords. But there at once was vengeance
Paid to the vikings, for I heard that Edward
Struck one of them so fiercely with his sword,
Restraining not the stroke, that at his feet
The fated warrior fell to the earth.
For this his prince, as soon as he had time,
Gave grateful thanks to his bold chamberlain.
So the stout-hearted warriors stood firm
In battle, and the young men eagerly
Competed who might first with point of spear
Deprive a fated soldier of his life;
And all around the slaughtered fell to earth.
Steadfast they stood, as Byrhtnoth stirred them on
Bade every soldier concentrate on war
Who wished to win renown against the Danes.

130 Wōd þā wīges heard,   wǣpen up āhōf,
bord tō gebeorge,   and wið þæs beornes stōp;
ēode swā ānrǣd   eorl tō þām ceorle;
ǣgþer hyra ōðrum   yfeles hogode.
Sende ðā se sǣrinc   sūþerne gār,
135 þæt gewundod wearð   wigena hlāford.
Hē scēaf þā mid ðām scylde   þæt se scēaft tōbærst,
and þæt spere sprengde   þæt hit sprang ongēan.
Gegremod wearð se gūðrinc;   hē mid gāre stang
wlancne wīcing   þe him þā wunde forgeaf.
140 Frōd wæs se fyrdrinc,   hē lēt his francan wadan
þurh ðæs hysses hals,   hand wīsode
þæt hē on þām fǣrsceaðan   feorh gerǣhte.
Ðā hē ōþerne   ofstlīce scēat
þæt sēo byrne tōbærst;   hē wæs on brēostum wund
145 þurh ðā hringlocan;   him æt heortan stōd
ǣtterne ord.   Se eorl wæs þē blīþra,
hlōh þā mōdi man,   sǣde Metode þanc
ðæs dægweorces   þe him Drihten forgeaf.
Forlēt þā drenga sum   daroð of handa,
150 flēogan of folman,   þæt se tō forð gewāt
þurh ðone æþelan   Æþelredes þegen.
Him be healfe stōd   hyse unweaxen,
cniht on gecampe,   se full cāflīce
brǣd of þām beorne   blōdigne gār,
155 Wulfstānes bearn,   Wulfmǣr se geonga,
forlēt forheardne   faran eft ongēan;
ord in gewōd,   þæt se on eorþan læg
þe his þēoden ǣr   þearle gerǣhte.
Ēode þā gesyrwed   secg tō þām eorle;
160 hē wolde þæs beornes   bēagas gefecgan,
rēaf and hringas   and gerēnod swurd.

130–2. Only the context shows that *wiges heard* is the *ceorle* and thus a viking, and *beornes* refers to Byrhtnoþ.

134. *superne*, 'southern, of southern make'. Frankish spears were popular, and the word itself was adopted for a spear as in ll. 77, 140, *francan*,

A warlike viking soldier then advanced,
His weapon raised, his shield up in defence,
And strode towards the earl, who in return
Marched resolutely forth to meet the churl.
They each intended evil to the other.
The seaman hurled a Frankish javelin
So that the leader of the troops was wounded.
He thrust out with his shield so that the shaft
Was shattered and the spear sprang back again.
Enraged, the hero seized his spear and stabbed
The proud, rash viking who had wounded him.
No novice was the earl, he made his spear
Pass through the young man's neck, guided his hand
So that he pierced the pirate fatally.
Then speedily he shot another man
So that his corslet cracked and through the chainmail
His breast was wounded, and the deadly point
Stood at his heart. This made the earl more glad;
The bold man laughed, and said thanks to the Lord
For the day's work that God had granted him.
A pirate hurled a dart then from his hand
So that it pierced Ethelred's noble thane.
Beside him stood a lad not fully grown,
A boy in battle, who right bravely drew
The bloody spear out of the warrior's wound.
He was the son of Wulfstan, young Wulfmar.
He threw the hardened weapon back again;
Its point passed in, and he lay on the ground
Who had before so sorely hurt his prince.
A well-armed viking then approached the earl,
He planned to take possession of his rings,
His ornate sword and all his other booty.

Þā Byrhtnōð brǣd   bill of scēðe,
brād and brūneccg,   and on þā byrnan slōh.
Tō raþe hine gelette   lidmanna sum

165 þā hē þæs eorles   earm āmyrde.
Fēoll þā tō foldan   fealohilte swurd,
ne mihte hē gehealdan   heardne mēce,
wǣpnes wealdan.   Þā gȳt þæt word gecwæð
hār hilderinc,   hyssas bylde,

170 bæd gangan forð   gōde gefēran;
ne mihte þā on fōtum leng   fæste gestandan.
Hē tō heofenum wlāt;
'Ic geþancie Þē,   ðēoda Waldend,
ealra þǣra wynna   þe ic on worulde gebād;

175 nū ic āh, milde Metod,   mǣste þearfe
þæt Þū mīnum gāste   gōdes geunne,
þæt mīn sāwul tō Đē   sīðian mōte
on Þīn geweald,   Þēoden engla,
mid friþe ferian.   Ic eom frymdi tō Þē

180 þæt hī helsceaðan   hȳnan ne mōton.'
Đā hine hēowon   hǣðene scealcas,
and bēgen þā beornas   þe him big stōdon,
Ælfnōð and Wulmǣr   bēgen lāgon,
ðā onemn hyra frēan   feorh gesealdon.

185 Hī bugon þā fram beaduwe   þe þǣr bēon noldon.
Þǣr wurdon Oddan bearn   ǣrest on flēame,
Godrīc fram gūþe,   and þone gōdan forlēt
þe him mænigne oft   mear gesealde.
Hē gehlēop þone eoh   þe āhte his hlāford,

190 on þām gerǣdum   þe hit riht ne wæs,
and his brōðru mid him   bēgen ærndon,
Godwine and Godwīg   gūþe ne gȳmdon,
ac wendon fram þām wīge   and þone wudu sōhton,

---

172. One half-line is apparently missing, though the transcript of the
MS has no gap. See too *Dream of Rood* l. 76 and *Seafarer* l. 16, both pre-
sumably accidental omissions. In *Wulf and Eadwacer* there are four clearly
intentional cases. In the translation I have added 'humbly made his prayer'.

Then Byrhtnoth drew his broad and bright-edged sword
Out of its sheath, and smote upon his corslet.
Too fast one of the pirates hindered him,
Smashing the earl's right arm. So fell to earth
The golden-hilted sword. Now could the earl
No longer hold the weapon or make use
Of his sharp sword. But still he urged them on,
The grey-haired chief encouraged the young men,
Told them to carry on in fellowship.
He could not stand firm on his feet much longer.
He looked to heaven, humbly made his prayer:
'I wish to thank You, Ruler of the nations,
For all the earthly joys that I have had.
And now, mild God, I have most need that You
Should grant grace to my spirit, that my soul
May come to You, into Your power, O Prince
Of angels, journey forth in peace. I pray
You will not let the devils harm my soul.'
Then heathen soldiers cut him to the earth,
And both the warriors who stood beside him,
Alfnoth and Wulfmar both lay on the ground,
Gave up their lives beside their prince and lord.
They then departed from the battlefield
Who did not wish to be there: Odda's sons
Were first in flight, as Godrich quit the field
And left the hero who so frequently
Had given him a horse. He leapt upon
The very steed his lord had owned, his saddle,
Which was not right at all, and both his brothers
Godwin and Godwig galloped after him.
They did not care for war, but turned away
And sought the woods, fled to a safer place

flugon on þæt fæsten   and hyra fēore burgon,
195 and manna mā   þonne hit ǣnig mǣð wǣre,
gyf hī þā geearnunga   ealle gemundon
þe hē him tō duguþe   gedōn hæfde;
swā him Offa on dæg   ǣr āsǣde
on þām meþelstede   þā hē gemōt hæfde,
200 þæt þǣr mōdiglīce   manega sprǣcon
þe eft æt þearfe   þolian noldon.
    Þā wearð āfeallen   þæs folces ealdor,
Æþelredes eorl;   ealle gesāwon
heorðgenēatas   þæt hyra heorra læg.
205 Þā ðǣr wendon forð   wlance þegenas,
unearge men   efston georne;
hī woldon þā ealle   ōðer twēga,
līf forlǣtan   oððe lēofne gewrecan.
    Swā hī bylde forð   bearn Ælfrīces,
210 wiga wintrum geong,   wordum mǣlde,
Ælfwine þā cwæð,   hē on ellen spræc:
'Gemunað þāra mǣla   þe wē oft æt meodo sprǣcon,
þonne wē on bence   bēot āhōfon,
hæleð on healle,   ymbe heard gewinn.
215 Nū mæg cunnian   hwā cēne sȳ.
Ic wylle mīne æþelo   eallum gecȳþan,
þæt ic wæs on Myrcon   miccles cynnes;
wæs mīn ealda fæder   Ealhelm hāten,
wīs ealdorman,   woruldgesǣlig.
220 Ne sceolon mē on þǣre þēode   þegenas ætwītan
þæt ic of ðisse fyrde   fēran wille,
eard gesēcan,   nū mīn ealdor ligeð
forhēawen æt hilde.   Mē is þæt hearma mǣst;
hē wæs ǣgðer mīn mǣg   and mīn hlāford.'
225 Þā hē forð ēode,   fǣhðe gemunde,
þæt hē mid orde   ānne gerǣhte
flotan on þām folce   þæt se on foldan læg
forwegen mid his wǣpne.   Ongan þā winas manian,
frȳnd and gefēran,   þæt hī forð ēodon.

62

And saved their lives, and many soldiers more
Than should have done if they had called to mind
The many kindnesses that he had shown them.
So Offa warned him in the meeting-place,
That very day, when he had held his council,
That many there spoke boldly who at need
Would not endure. Then was the leader fallen,
Ethelred's earl, and all his household saw
Their prince lie slain. Then gallant thanes went forth,
Men hastened eagerly who were not cowards.
They all intended one of two results;
To lose their lives or to avenge their dear one.
Thus Alfwin son of Alfrich urged them on,
A hero young in years addressed them boldly:
'Remember all the speeches that we uttered
Often when drinking mead, when we made vows
Upon the benches, heroes in the hall,
About hard strife. Now may whoever has
True courage show it. Here will I reveal
My genealogy to all. I come
From a great family in Mercia;
Alderman Ealhelm was my grandfather,
Wise, prosperous, and honoured in this world.
The thanes among that race shall not reproach me
That I intend to leave this troop and go
Home to my land now that my lord lies dead,
Cut down in battle. My grief is the greatest,
For he was both my kinsman and my lord.'
Then he advanced, and set his mind on war,
Until among that host he stabbed a sailor
With spear-point, so that to the ground he fell
Killed by his weapon. He encouraged all
His colleagues, friends and comrades to advance.

230 Offa gemælde,   æscholt āscēoc:
'Hwæt þū, Ælfwine,   hafast ealle gemanode
þegenas tō þearfe;   nū ūre þēoden liд,
eorl on eorдan,   ūs is eallum þearf
þæt ūre æghwylc   ōþerne bylde
235 wigan tō wīge,   þā hwīle þe hē wǣpen mæge
habban and healdan,   heardne mēce,
gār and gōd swurd.   Ūs Godrīc hæfд,
earh Oddan bearn,   ealle beswicene;
wēnde þæs formoni man,   þā hē on mēare rād,
240 on wlancan þām wicge,   þæt wǣre hit ūre hlāford.
For þan wearд hēr on felda   folc tōtwǣmed,
scyldburh tōbrocen.   Ābrēoдe his angin,
þæt hē hēr swā manigne   man āflȳmde.'
Lēofsunu gemælde   and his linde āhōf,
245 bord tō gebeorge;   hē þām beorne oncwæд:
'Ic þæt gehāte   þæt ic heonon nelle
flēon fōtes trym,   ac wille furдor gān,
wrecan on gewinne   mīnne winedrihten.
Ne þurfon mē embe Stūrmere   stedefæste hælæд
250 wordum ætwītan,   nū mīn wine gecranc,
þæt ic hlāfordlēas   hām sīдie,
wende fram wīge;   ac mē sceal wǣpen niman,
ord and īren.'   Hē ful yrre wōd,
feaht fæstlīce,   flēam hē forhogode.
255 Dunnere þā cwæд,   daroд ācwehte,
unorne ceorl,   ofer eall clypode,
bæd þæt beorna gehwylc   Byrhtnōд wrǣce:
'Ne mæg nā wandian   se þe wrecan þenceд
frēan on folce,   ne for fēore murnan.'
260 Þā hī forд ēodon,   fēores hī ne rōhton.
Ongunnon þā hīredmen   heardlīce feohtan,
grame gārberend,   and God bǣdon

236–7. Compressed in translation.

Then Offa spoke, and shook his ash-wood spear:
'Alfwin, you have encouraged all the thanes
In time of need. Now that our prince, our earl,
Lies on the ground the need for all is great
That each of us should urge on every other
Soldier to battle, for as long as he
May hold and keep his weapons, his sharp spear
And trusty sword. Godrich the coward son
Of Odda has been traitor to us all.
When he rode on that horse, on that proud steed,
Full many a man thought that it was our lord.
Thus was our force divided in the field,
The shield-wall broken. May he come to grief,
That he put here so many men to flight.'
Leofsunu spoke, he raised his linden-shield
Aloft, and answered thus that warrior:
'I promise this, that I will not from here
Flee one foot's space, but rather will go forward,
Avenge my lord and patron in the throng.
No cause shall steadfast men of Sturmere have
To blame me with their words now that my prince
Lies dead, that I shall lordless travel home,
Turn from the fight. Rather shall weapons take me,
Spear-point and blade.' He went full angry on,
Fought with tenacity and scorned to flee.
Then Dunnere spoke out, brandished his dart,
A simple churl, he called out over all,
Said every man should take revenge for Byrhtnoth:
'He who among this people would avenge
His lord must weaken not nor care for life.'
So they advanced, and cared not for their lives.
The household troop then started fighting fiercely,
Furious spearmen, and they prayed to God

þæt hī mōston gewrecan   hyra winedrihten
and on hyra fēondum   fyl gewyrcan.
265 Him se gȳsel ongan   geornlīce fylstan;
hē wæs on Norðhymbron   heardes cynnes,
Ecglāfes bearn,   him wæs Æscferð nama.
Hē ne wandode nā   æt þām wīgplegan,
ac hē fȳsde forð   flān genehe;
270 hwīlon hē on bord scēat,   hwīlon beorn tǣsde;
ǣfre embe stunde   hē sealde sume wunde
þā hwīle ðe hē wǣpna   wealdan mōste.
    Þā gȳt on orde stōd   Ēadweard se langa,
gearo and geornful;   gylpwordum spræc
275 þæt hē nolde flēogan   fōtmǣl landes,
ofer bæc būgan,   þā his betera leg.
Hē bræc þone bordweall   and wið þā beornas feaht,
oð þæt hē his sincgyfan   on þām sǣmannum
wurðlīce wrec,   ǣr hē on wæle lǣge.
280 Swā dyde Æþerīc,   æþele gefēra,
fūs and forðgeorn,   feaht eornoste,
Sībyrhtes brōðor   and swīðe mænig ōþer
clufon cellod bord,   cēne hī weredon.
Bǣrst bordes lærig,   and sēo byrne sang
285 gryrelēoða sum.   Þā æt gūðe slōh
Offa þone sǣlidan   þæt hē on eorðan fēoll,
and ðǣr Gaddes mǣg   grund gesōhte;
raðe wearð æt hilde   Offa forhēawen.
Hē hæfde ðēah geforþod   þæt hē his frēan gehēt,
290 swa hē bēotode ǣr   wið his bēahgifan,
þæt hī sceoldon bēgen   on burh rīdan,
hāle tō hāme,   oððe on here crincgan,
on wælstōwe   wundum sweltan.
Hē læg ðegenlīce   ðēodne gehende.

283. *cellod* is only found here, and its meaning is unknown.
284. 'smitten' added in translation.

That they might take revenge for their loved lord,
Achieve the slaughter of their enemies.
The hostage started eagerly to help them.
He was of bold Northumbrian family,
The son of Edglaf, Ashferth was his name.
He never weakened in the battle-play,
But sent forth darts fast and continuously.
Sometimes he struck a shield, sometimes he pierced
A man, and constantly he gave some wound,
As long as he survived to wield his weapons.
Edward the tall still stood among the troop,
Ready and eager; he spoke vaunting words
That he would never flee a foot of land,
Retreat at all, now that his lord lay dead.
He broke the ranks and fought against those men
Until he had avenged his patron nobly
Among their foes before he too lay dead.
Likewise did Atherich, a valiant comrade,
Forceful and keen; the brother of Sibirht
Fought earnestly, and very many others,
They cleft the rounded shield, and boldly strove.
The shield's rim burst, the smitten corslet sang
A doleful dirge. Then Offa struck in battle
A seaman so that to the earth he fell;
There too Gad's kinsman tumbled to the ground,
Offa was quickly cut down in the throng;
Nevertheless he had fulfilled the vow
Which he had made his generous ring-giver,
That either they should both ride back to town,
Go home unharmed, or die among that army,
Perish of wounds upon the battle-field.
He lay like true retainer by his lord.

295 Ðā wearð borda gebræc.   Brimmen wōdon
    gūðe gegremode;   gār oft þurhwōd
    fǣges feorhhūs.   Forð ðā ēode Wīstān,
    Þurstānes sunu   wið þās secgas feaht.
    Hē wæs on geþrange   hyra þrēora bana
300 ǣr him Wīgelmes bearn   on þām wæle lǣge.
    Þǣr wæs stīð gemōt;   stōdon fæste
    wigan on gewinne;   wīgend cruncon,
    wundum wērige,   wæl fēol on eorþan.
    Ōswold and Ēadwold   ealle hwīle,
305 bēgen þā gebrōþru,   beornas trymedon,
    hyra winemāgas   wordon bǣdon
    þæt hī þǣr æt ðearfe   þolian sceoldon,
    unwāclīce   wǣpna nēotan.
    Byrhtwold maþelode,   bord hafenode,
310 se wæs eald genēat,   æsc ācwehte,
    hē ful baldlīce   beornas lǣrde:
    'Hige sceal þē heardra,   heorte þē cēnre,
    mōd sceal þē māre,   þē ūre mægen lȳtlað.
    Hēr līð ūre ealdor   eall forhēawen,
315 gōd on grēote;   ā mæg gnornian
    se ðe nū fram þis wīgplegan   wendan þenceð.
    Ic eom frōd fēores;   fram ic ne wille,
    ac ic mē be healfe   mīnum hlāforde,
    be swā lēofan men   licgan þence.'
320 Swā hī Æþelgāres bearn   ealle bylde,
    Godrīc tō gūþe.   Oft hē gār forlēt,
    wælspere windan   on þā wīcingas,
    swā hē on þām folce   fyrmest ēode,
    hēow and hȳnde   oð þæt hē on hilde gecranc.
325 Næs þæt nā se Godrīc   þe ðā gūðe forbēah.

297–300. Wistan seems clearly to be the son of Þurstan and therefore can
scarcely be also the son of Wigelm. The least implausible explanation is
that Offa, whose death has just been described in ll. 285–94, and who
seems to have become the leader on Byrhtnoþ's death, was the son of
Wigelm.

There was a clash of shields. The Vikings came,
Enraged by battle. Many a spear passed through
The life-house of the doomed. Wistan went forth,
The son of Thurstan fought against those men.
Already in the throng he had slain three
Before the son of Wigelm fell in death.
That was a fierce encounter. Warriors
Stood fast in battle, though their comrades fell
Weary with wounds. Dead men dropped to the earth.
All this time Oswold and his brother Eadwold
Inspired the warriors, and bade their kinsmen
That in that grim necessity they should
Endure and use their weapons without weakness.
Byrhtwold spoke out, he raised his shield aloft
And shook his spear; an elderly retainer,
Courageously he taught the warriors:
'Mind must be harder, spirit must be bolder,
And heart the greater, as our might grows less.
Here lies our leader in the dust, the hero
Cut down in battle. Ever must he mourn
Who thinks to go home from this battle-play.
I am an aged man. Hence will I not,
But I intend to die beside my lord,
Give up my life beside so dear a chief.'
So too did Godrich, son of Athelgar,
Encourage them to war. Often he hurled
A murderous spear among the viking host.
Thus foremost he advanced among the people.
He slashed and smote, until he died in battle.
But that was not the Godrich who had fled.

The Wife's Lament

Detailed interpretation of this poem has given a lot of trouble. A woman is speaking, and her story seems to be this: she is compelled to live in an unpleasant place while her husband has been exiled overseas as a result of some crime by her husband connected with his kinsmen, who had been opposed to the woman and her marriage. Even this much is not universally agreed, and it must be admitted that according to any interpretation the speaker appears to have little regard to the chronology of the events described. If however we accept that the above is the general framework, we may tentatively add that ll. 15–17 mean that she is a foreigner. She has come from abroad to marry but her husband's kinsmen disapprove. Despite his cheerful demeanour her husband secretly plans and executes some crime as a result of which he is banished and she condemned to the earth-hall. This is substantially the view of the latest editor, R. F. Leslie, and seems the best. However the word *ǣrest*, l. 6, remains an objection to this theory.

BIBLIOGRAPHY

Kershaw

ASPR III

R. F. Leslie, *Three Old English Elegies*, Manchester, 1961

K. Malone, 'Two English *Frauenlieder*', *Comparative Literature*, XIV, 1962

J. L. Curry, 'Approaches to a Translation of the Anglo-Saxon *The Wife's Lament*', *Medium Ævum*, XXXV, 1966

The Wife's Lament

Ic þis giedd wrece   bi mē ful gēomorre,
mīnre sylfre sīð.   Ic þæt secgan mæg
hwæt ic yrmþa gebād,   siþþan ic up wēox,
nīwes oþþe ealdes,   nō mā þonne nū.
5   Ā ic wīte wonn   mīnra wræcsīþa.
   Ǣrest mīn hlāford gewāt   heonan of lēodum
ofer ȳþa gelāc;   hæfde ic ūhtceare
hwǣr mīn lēodfruma   londes wǣrc.
   Ðā ic mē fēran gewāt   folgað sēcan,
10   winelēas wrǣcca   for mīnre wēaþearfe,
ongunnon þæt þæs monnes   māgas hycgan
þurh dyrne geþōht   þæt hȳ tōdǣlden unc,
þæt wit gewīdost   in woruldrīce
lifdon lāðlicost;   and mec longade.
15   Hēt mec hlāford mīn   hēr eard niman;
āhte ic lēofra lȳt   on þissum londstede,
holdra frēonda;   forþon is mīn hyge gēomor.
   Ðā ic mē ful gemæcne   monnan funde,
heardsǣligne,   hygegēomorne,
20   mōd mīþendne,   morþor hycgendne,
blīþe gebǣro.   Ful oft wit bēotedan
þæt unc ne gedǣlde   nemne dēað āna,
ōwiht elles;   eft is þæt onhworfen,
is nū fornumen   swā hit nō wǣre
25   frēondscipe uncer.   Sceal ic feor ge nēah
mīnes felalēofan   fǣhðu drēogan.
   Heht mec mon wunian   on wuda bearwe,

---

15. *her eard*, MS *herheard*. This is an important crux, as the meaning given to this half-line affects the interpretation of the whole poem. The main suggestions are: (i) *herheard* is a form of *hearg-eard* meaning 'dwelling in a grove' or 'sanctuary' (see Kershaw p. 173); (ii) divide into *her heard*, taking *heard* either as an adjective meaning 'cruel' (see Kershaw as above) or as an adverb; (iii) omit the second *h* and translate *eard niman* as 'take up an abode'. This proposal gives better sense and less improbable syntax.

The Wife's Lament

I sing this song about myself, full sad,
My own distress, and tell what hardships I
Have had to suffer since I first grew up,
Present and past, but never more than now;
I ever suffered grief through banishment.
For since my lord departed from this people
Over the sea, each dawn have I had care
Wondering where my lord may be on land.
When I set off to join and serve my lord,
A friendless exile in my sorry plight,
My husband's kinsmen plotted secretly
How they might separate us from each other
That we might live in wretchedness apart
Most widely in the world: and my heart longed.
In the first place my lord had ordered me
To take up my abode here, though I had
Among these people few dear loyal friends;
Therefore my heart is sad. Then had I found
A fitting man, but one ill-starred, distressed,
Whose hiding heart was contemplating crime,
Though cheerful his demeanour. We had vowed
Full many a time that nought should come between us
But death alone, and nothing else at all.
All that has changed, and it is now as though
Our marriage and our love had never been,
And far or near forever I must suffer
The feud of my beloved husband dear.
So in this forest grove they made me dwell,

under āctrēo in þām eorðscræfe.

Eald is þes eorðsele, eal ic eom oflongad;
30 sindon dena dimme, dūna uphēa,
bitre burgtūnas brērum beweaxne,
wīc wynna lēas. Ful oft mec hēr wrāþe begeaṭ
fromsīþ frēan. Frȳnd sind on eorþan,
lēofe lifgende, leger weardiað,
35 þonne ic on ūhtan āna gonge
under āctrēo geond þās eorðscrafu.
Þǣr ic sittan mōt sumorlangne dæg,
þǣr ic wēpan mæg mīne wræcsīþas,
earfoþa fela; forþon ic ǣfre ne mæg
40 þǣre mōdceare mīnre gerestan
ne ealles þæs longaþes þe mec on þissum līfe begeat.
Ā scyle geong mon wesan gēomormōd,
heard heortan geþōht; swylce habban sceal
blīþe gebǣro, ēac þon brēostceare,
45 sinsorgna gedreag; sȳ æt him sylfum gelong
eal his worulde wyn. Sȳ ful wīde fāh
feorres folclondes þæt mīn frēond siteð
under stānhliþe storme behrīmed,
wine wērigmōd, wætre beflōwen
50 on drēorsele, drēogeð se mīn wine
micle mōdceare; hē gemon tō oft
wynlicran wīc. Wā bið þām þe sceal
of langoþe lēofes ābīdan.

45–7. The gnomic passage from l. 42 is appropriate in the general scheme
of the poem, but the relationship of the two 'sy . . .' clauses has given much
difficulty. No solution so far offered is convincing. There is probably a
major scribal blunder.

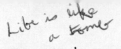

Life is like a tomb

Under the oak-tree, in this earthy barrow.
Old is this earth-cave, all I do is yearn.
The dales are dark with high hills up above,
Sharp hedge surrounds it, overgrown with briars,

place of death

And joyless is the place. Full often here
The absence of my lord comes sharply to me.
Dear lovers in this world lie in their beds,
While I alone at crack of dawn must walk
Under the oak-tree round this earthy cave,
Where I must stay the length of summer days,
Where I may weep my banishment and all
My many hardships, for I never can
Contrive to set at rest my careworn heart,
Nor all the longing that this life has brought me.
A young man always must be serious,
And tough his character; likewise he should

speaker at end of soliloquy

Seem cheerful, even though his heart is sad
With multitude of cares. All earthly joy
Must come from his own self. Since my dear lord
Is outcast, far off in a distant land,
Frozen by storms beneath a stormy cliff
And dwelling in some desolate abode
Beside the sea, my weary-hearted lord
Must suffer pitiless anxiety.
And all too often he will call to mind
A happier dwelling. Grief must always be
For him who yearning longs for his beloved.

The Husband's Message

The general situation in the poem is perfectly clear. Two problems are however still the subject of debate. First, does the poem start with Riddle 60, which comes immediately before it in the manuscript? (For Riddle 60 see p. 106.) The answer to this depends largely on whether one considers that the rest is spoken by a human messenger or a personified rune-stave, a device of which the Anglo-Saxons were quite capable (see *Metrical Preface to the Pastoral Care*, p. 130).

The second problem is what the runes in ll. 50–1 signify. Runes were the letters of an ancient Germanic alphabet, ultimately derived from the Mediterranean alphabets, which was used for carving on wood or stone and which to some extent survived the introduction of writing. Each rune (with minor exceptions) had a name which was a word beginning with the sound it represented, and the runes could therefore be used for punning statements. Thus the poet Cynewulf signed his poems by closing with a passage which contained the names of the runes which spelt his name. In this case there are two attractive solutions offered. These runes stand for *Sigel*, 'sun', *Rad*, 'road', *EAr*, either 'earth' or 'water', *Wynn*, 'joy', *Mann* or *Dæg*, 'man' or 'day'. E. A. Kock proposes that the runes represent three objects by which oaths were commonly sworn, the sky (sun-road), the earth (earth-joy), and the swearer himself (man). R. W. V. Elliott suggests that the runes summarise the whole poem, hence either: 'Follow the sun's path across the sea and ours will be joy and the happiness and prosperity of the bright day;' or: 'Follow the sun's path across the sea to find joy with the man who is waiting for you.'

BIBLIOGRAPHY

Editions as for *Wife's Lament*

E. A. Kock, 'Interpretations and Emendations of Early English Texts', *Anglia*, XLV, 1921

R. W. V. Elliott, 'The Runes in *The Husband's Message*', *Journal of English and Germanic Philology*, LIV, 1955

Nū ic onsundran   þē secgan wille
.... trēocyn   ic tūdre āwēox;
in mec ælda ......   sceal ellor londes
settan ....   sealte strēamas
5 ....   Ful oft ic on bātes
.... gesōhte
þǣr mec mondryhten   mīn ......
ofer hēah hafu;   eom nū hēr cumen
on cēolþele,   and nū cunnan sceal
10 hū þū ymb mōdlufan   mīnes frēan
on hyge hycge.   Ic gehātan dear
þæt þū þǣr tīrfæste   trēowe findest.

Hwæt, þec þonne biddan hēt   se þisne bēam āgrōf
þæt þū sinchroden   sylf gemunde
15 on gewitlocan   wordbēotunga
þe git on ǣrdagum   oft gesprǣcon,
þenden git mōston   on meoduburgum
eard weardigan,   ān lond būgan,
frēondscype fremman.   Hine fǣhþo ādrāf
20 of sigeþēode.   Heht nū sylfa þē
lustum lǣran,   þæt þū lagu drēfde,
siþþan þū gehȳrde   on hliþes ōran
galan gēomorne   gēac on bearwe.
Ne lǣt þū þec siþþan   sīþes getwǣfan,
25 lāde gelettan   lifgendne monn.
Ongin mere sēcan,   mǣwes ēþel,
onsite sǣnacan,   þæt þū sūð heonan
ofer merelāde   monnan findest,
þǣr se þēoden is   þīn on wēnum.
30 Ne mæg him on worulde   willa gelimpan
māra on gemyndum,   þæsþe hē mē sægde,

1–6. The MS is badly damaged at this point. My text is a compromise
between Leslie and ASPR, and the translation is largely guess-work.

The Husband's Message

Now will I tell to you who live apart *isolated one*
How I grew up in youth among the trees.
On me must sons of men write messages,
Send me from foreign lands across the waves,
Thus guide their thoughts across the salty streams.
Often by boat have I sought out some land
Where my lord sent me forth to take some message
Over the deep wide sea; now have I come
On shipboard here, and now must I find out
How you feel in your heart about your love
Towards my lord. For I dare promise you
That you will find great loyalty in him.
He bids me tell you, then, who carved this wood,
That you, bejewelled, should yourself recall
In your own secret heart the vows and oaths
That you both made in former times together,
When you might still together live among
The festive cities, both dwell in one land,
And love each other. Feud drove him away
From this great people. Now he orders me
Himself to urge you joyfully to cross
The sea when at the hill-side's edge you hear
The cuckoo singing sad amid the grove.
Do not let any living man deter you
From travelling or stay you from the journey.
Go to the sea, the country of the gull,
And board a ship, that you may southwards thence
Rejoin your man across the water's ways,
There where your lord is waiting for your coming.
For in the world no stronger wish could come
Into his heart, he told me so himself,

þonne inc geunne   alwaldend God
þæt git ætsomne   siþþan mōtan
secgum and gesīþum   sinc brytnian,
35 næglede bēagas;   hē genōh hafað
fædan goldes . . . .
þæt he mid elþēode   ēþel healde,
fægre foldan . . . .
holdra hæleþa,   þēah þe hēr mīn wine
. . . .
40 nȳde gebæded,   nacan ūt āþrong,
and on ȳþa gelagu   āna sceolde
faran on flotweg,   forðsīþes georn,
mengan merestrēamas.   Nū se mon hafað
wēan oferwunnen;   nis him wilna gād,
45 ne mēara ne māðma   ne meododrēama
ænges ofer eorþan   eorlgestrēona,
þēodnes dohtor,   gif hē þīn beneah.
Ofer eald gebēot   incer twēga,
gehȳre ic ætsomne   .S.R. geador
50 .EA.W. and .M.   āþe benemnan,
þæt hē þā wære   and þā winetrēowe
be him lifgendum   læstan wolde
þe git on ærdagum   oft gespræconn.

33–41. The MS is again damaged. Some words and letters are here supplied following various editors. For full details see ASPR and Leslie. Much of the translation is guessed at.

41. *gelagu*, following Leslie, the MS being illegible.

Than that almighty God should grant you both
That you may distribute together treasures
And well-made rings to comrades and retainers.
He has in his possession burnished gold
Enough for him to hold a fine estate
Among the foreign people noble land
And loyal warriors, though here my lord
Compelled by need pushed out his boat and left,
And had to cross the rolling waves alone,
Sail on the sea, and, anxious to depart,
Stir up the water ways. Now has this man
Conquered his woes; he lacks not what he wants,
Horses or treasures or the joys of hall,
Or any noble treasure in this world,
O prince's daughter, if he may have you.
About the former vows between you both,
I understand he coupled in his oath
Heaven and earth, and joined thereto himself
That he would keep, as long as he has life,
Truly with you the bond and pledge of faith
Which you made frequently in former days.

lord as husband
lord as god

Wulf and Eadwacer

I use the generally accepted title of this attractive but almost totally obscure poem, though as will be seen it seems to me inappropriate. It was early regarded as a riddle, but this now appears quite unacceptable. Ingenious attempts have been made to relate it to one or other of the known Germanic stories, as has happened to *The Wife's Lament* and *The Husband's Message*, and some scholars have also tried to link these three poems or combinations of these and others together. None of these theories is at all persuasive. It is clear that a lady is speaking, and that she addresses a character as Wulf and another as Eadwacer. The critics have variously cast them as husband and lover. I do not believe it is possible to reconstruct the story, though I now offer my own solution. The *lāc*, l. 1, is the lady's pregnancy by a raider from the other island brought about during some raid. Her people want vengeance. She calls her lover *Wulf* because he was a raider, compare *The Battle of Maldon*, l. 96, where the Viking raiders are called *wælwulfas*. Their brief encounter is brilliantly described, with a masterly paradox in the recalling of her feelings, l. 12, and the power of evocation in the passage is increased when she tells of her longing for her lover's presence, ll. 13–15. *Hwelp*, l. 16, must surely be a punning reference to a child of *Wulf*, whom ironically a wolf is bearing or shall bear to the wood, which may be a reference to the child's impending death, perhaps to be brought about by the lady's kinsfolk to whom this birth is unwanted. If this interpretation is anywhere near the truth, it seems that there is no-one except Wulf whom the lady would be likely to address at this time, and particularly in such terms, so my proposal is that Eadwacer is the real name of Wulf. It may be significant that the dual pronoun *uncerne* immediately follows the name *Ēadwacer*, and it might therefore contextually imply that the two people meant are the lady and Eadwacer, in which case the point of *hwelp* as a pun would be lost if he were a different person. This proposal is however as unprovable as any of the others. What is beyond doubt is that the poignancy of expression of the lady's grief emerging through all the obscurities has still power to move.

BIBLIOGRAPHY

ASPR III

K. Malone, 'Two English *Frauenlieder*', *Comparative Literature*, XIV, 1962

Wulf and Eadwacer

Lēodum is mīnum   swylce him mon lāc gife;
willað hȳ hine āþecgan,   gif hē on þrēat cymeð.
Ungelīc is ūs.
Wulf is on īege,   ic on ōþerre.
5 Fæst is þæt ēglond,   fenne biworpen.
Sindon wælrēowe   weras þǣr on īge;
willað hȳ hine āþecgan,   gif hē on þrēat cymeð.
Ungelīce is ūs.
Wulfes ic mīnes wīdlāstum   wēnum dogode;
10 þonne hit wæs rēnig weder   and ic reotugu sæt,
þonne mec se beaducāfa   bōgum bilegde,
wæs mē wyn tō þon,   wæs mē hwæþre ēac lāð.
Wulf, mīn Wulf,   wēna mē þīne
sēoce gedydon,   þīne seldcymas,
15 murnende mōd,   nāles metelīste.
Gehȳrest þū, Ēadwacer?   Uncerne earmne hwelp
bireð wulf tō wuda.
Þæt mon ēaþe tōslīteð   þætte nǣfre gesomnad wæs,
uncer giedd geador.

---

16. earmne, MS earne. The MS reading suggests the adjective *earh*,
'cowardly'. It is contextually better (or perhaps better fits my theory) to
read *earmne* from *earm*, 'wretched'.

19. *giedd*. Substitution of *gæd*, 'fellowship', has been proposed, but *giedd*
may be taken to imply poetically the relationship of marriage.

Wulf and Eadwacer

It is as though my people had been given
A present. They will wish to capture him
If he comes with a troop. We are apart.
Wulf is on one isle, I am on another.
Fast is that island set among the fens.
Murderous are the people who inhabit
That island. They will wish to capture him
If he comes with a troop. We are apart.
Grieved have I for my Wulf with distant longings.
Then was it rainy weather, and I sad,
When the bold warrior laid his arms about me.
I took delight in that and also pain.
O Wulf, my Wulf, my longing for your coming
Has made me ill, the rareness of your visits,
My grieving spirit, not the lack of food.
Eadwacer, do you hear me? For a wolf
Shall carry to the woods our wretched whelp.
Men very easily may put asunder
That which was never joined, our song together.

Song of Songs - Bible story of Bride
commenting of no show
groom

85

Deor

The general structure of this poem is clear enough. Five references are made to disastrous situations of a mythical or historical nature, each followed by the encouraging line of the refrain. The poet then goes on to reflect in Christian terms on the vicissitudes of life, after which he tells of another sad situation which he fictitiously attributes to himself. The poem ends with the optimistic re-statement of the refrain line. *Deor* shares some features with the longer poem *Widsiþ* which is also fictitious and in the first person. *Deor* refers allusively to a few well-known stories, *Widsiþ* does the same to a large number, though in most cases merely listing the names and nationalities of many important historical figures of Germanic story. It is possible that both poems are to be regarded as repertory pieces, poems with which a *scop* might introduce himself to a new audience and in so doing give a specimen of his art and at the same time imply the great extent of his *repertoire*. The constant harping in *Widsiþ* on the great generosity with which the fictitious narrator has been treated by great lords lends some support to this theory. Thus ll. 65–7 read: 'And I was ... among the Burgundians, where I received a ring. There Guðhere gave me a glorious treasure as a reward for song; that was no niggardly king.'

The stories told in *Deor* are discussed rather briefly by Kemp Malone in his edition, and most of them in more detail by R. W. Chambers in his edition of *Widsiþ*. The story of Weland, which covers the first two sections of the poem, was well-known in Old English, several references to him being made in *Beowulf* and elsewhere. He was the mythical smith-god, whom King Niðhad captured and made to work for him, having ham-strung him. He gained his revenge by killing the king's two sons and raping his daughter Beadohild, who became pregnant. In some versions of the story she gave birth to the well-known hero Widia, who became involved in various stories relating to Eormanric (see below). The various versions of the Weland story are well attested in Norse and continental accounts. The story of Geat and Mæðhild is obscure, but it appears from two recently recorded ballads, one Norwegian and one Icelandic, that Mæðhild dreamed that she was to drown in a river, and so it came about. Geat succeeded by the power of his harp in rescuing her from the water-demon. The story of Þeodric presents difficulties. It is not clear from the context whether he is to be pitied or his subjects. There are two candidates for this role, Theoderic the Frank (Kemp Malone's choice), and Theoderic the Goth, who ruled for thirty-three years at Ravenna, was a just and competent ruler, but was an Aryan heretic and responsible for the death of Boethius. He thus might well have been regarded as an evil tyrant by later Christians, and the thirty-three years is not far off the thirty of the poem. There is unfortunately no evidence to connect the name *Mæringa burg* with Ravenna, or indeed anywhere else. However on balance it seems that Chambers is right in believing that he is the king here referred to. Eormanric, king of the Goths at an important point in their history, who died *c.* 375, became an even more important figure in many Germanic stories, in some of which he emerged as the type of the cruel and treacherous tyrant. Heorrenda was a poet in a famous story who successfully assisted his king, Heoden, in the wooing of Hild. These stories are more adequately summarised by J. C. Pope, *Seven Old English Poems*, pp. 92–6.

The conventional nature of the philosophical passage, ll. 28–34, can be seen by comparison with a passage from *The Fortunes of Men*, ll. 64–7:

'Swā missenlīce   meahtig Dryhten
geond eorþan scēat   eallum dǣleð,
scyreþ ond scrīfeð   ond gesceapo healdeð,
sumum ēadwelan,   sumum earfeða dǣl . . .'

'So variously mighty God throughout the regions of the earth

shares out to all, He assigns and allots and holds men's destinies,
to one prosperity, to one a share of hardships. . . .'

BIBLIOGRAPHY

Kemp Malone, *Deor*, Methuen's Old English Library, London,
1933
ASPR III
Pope, 7 OE P
R. W. Chambers, *Widsith*, Cambridge, 1912.

Deor

Wēlund him be wurman   wræces cunnade,
ānhȳdig eorl   earfoþa drēag,
hæfde him tō gesīþþe   sorge and longaþ,
wintercealde wræce;   wēan oft onfond
5   siþþan hine Nīðhād on   nēde legde,
swoncre seonobende   on sȳllan monn.
Þæs oferēode,   þisses swā mæg.

Beadohilde ne wæs   hyre brōþra dēaþ
on sefan swā sār   swā hyre sylfre þing,
10   þæt hēo gearolīce   ongieten hæfde
þæt hēo ēacen wæs;   ǣfre ne meahte
þrīste geþencan   hū ymb þæt sceolde.
Þæs oferēode,   þisses swā mæg.

Wē þæt Mǣðhilde   mōne gefrugnon
15   wurdon grundlēase   Gēates frīge,
þæt hī sēo sorglufu   slǣp ealle binōm.
Þæs oferēode,   þisses swā mæg.

Ðēodric āhte   þrītig wintra
Mǣringa burg;   þæt wæs monegum cūþ.
20   Þæs oferēode,   þisses swā mæg.

1. *be wurman* has defied explanation. Some suggestions are: (i) that *wurman* would be the correct OE form for the Swedish tribe called the *Vermar*; but there is no reason to believe that Weland was connected with them; (ii) *wurman* is a form of *wyrmum*, 'serpents', which Malone suggests means 'swords', swords being frequently damascened in a snake-like pattern; compare *Judith* l. 222 where arrows are called *hildenædran*; this interpretation is contextually unconvincing; (iii) various substitutions for *wurman* have been offered, but none of these is satisfying.

12. *þriste*, 'firmly', omitted in translation, the rest being paraphrased.

14. *mone* MS *monge*. Sense of a sort can be made of the MS reading, but this tentative proposal of Malone gives a more convincing meaning.

Deor

Weland among the Wermas suffered woe,
High-minded lord, he went through torments long,
Sorrow and longing were his company,
Winter·cold exile. Hardship was his lot
After Nithhad with supple sinew-bonds
Condemned the better man to live in bondage.
That passed away, and so may this from me.

Beadohild grieved less for her brothers' death
Than for her own distress, when she perceived
That she was pregnant; she could not foresee
How that mishap could ever turn out well.
That passed away, and so may this from me.

We know that Meathhild the sad wife of Geat
Had endless cause for tears and lamentation.
Unhappy love deprived her of all sleep.
That passed away, and so may this from me.

Theodric ruled the city of the Mearings
For thirty years. That was well-known to many.
That passed away, and so may this from me.

refrains

We geāscodan   Eormanrīces
wylfenne geþōht;   āhte wīde folc
Gotena rīces.   Þæt wæs grim cyning.
Sæt secg monig   sorgum gebunden,
25   wēan on wēnan,   wȳscte geneahhe
þæt þæs cynerīces   ofercumen wǣre.
Þæs oferēode,   þisses swā mæg.

Siteð sorgcearig,   sǣlum bidǣled,
on sefan sweorceð,   sylfum þinceð
30   þæt sȳ endelēas   earfoða dǣl.
Mæg þonne geþencan,   þæt geond þās woruld
wītig Dryhten   wendeþ geneahhe,
eorle monegum   āre gescēawað,
wislīcne blǣd,   sumum wēana dǣl.
35   Þæt ic bi mē sylfum   secgan wille,
þæt ic hwīle wæs   Heodeninga scop,
dryhtne dȳre.   Mē wæs Dēor noma.
Āhte ic fela wintra   folgað tilne,
holdne hlāford,   oþþæt Heorrenda nū,
40   lēoðcræftig monn,   londryht geþāh,
þæt mē eorla hlēo   ǣr gesealde.
Þæs oferēode,   þisses swā mæg.

37. The preterite *wæs* is surprising; perhaps it merely stresses the ficti-
tious nature of the poet's attribution of the story to himself.

We have heard much about the wolvish mind
Of King Ermanaric who long controlled
The people of the Goths: a cruel king.
Many a man lived in the bonds of sorrow,
Expected nought but grief, wished constantly
That this dread kingdom might be overthrown.
That passed away, and so may this from me.

The anxious, grieving man, deprived of joy,
Lives with a darkened mind; it seems to him
His share of sorrows will be everlasting;
But he can think that in this world wise God
Brings change continually: to many a man
He offers grace, assured prosperity,
But others he assigns a share of woe.
About my own plight now I wish to speak:
Once I was minstrel of the Heodenings,
Dear to my patron, and my name was Deor.
I held for many years a fine position
And loyal lord, until Heorrenda now,
That skilful poet, has received my lands,
Which once my lord and master gave to me.
That passed away, and so may this from me.

Riddles

There are 95 riddles in the Exeter Book, several of which are incomplete, damaged, corrupt, or otherwise insoluble. They vary in length from four or five lines to over a hundred. The subject matter is very diverse, and may be roughly divided into the religious, the obscene, and the descriptive of natural or domestic objects and weapons. The few obscene ones consist of the joke of describing some apparently obscene object which in fact turns out to represent something else. The more general descriptive type can be further divided into those which are more concerned with the beauty and interest of the object involved and those more interested in the ingenuity, often verbal, of the riddle. The latter may be illustrated by *Riddle 23*, which begins: *Agof is min noma eft onhwyrfed*, where *Agof* is for *Agob*, which when reversed gives *Boga*, 'bow'.

From the fifth century the riddle became a popular Latin exercise. Its great period in England was the eighth century, when it was practised by Bishop Aldhelm, Archbishop Tatwine and others. There is no homogeneity about the Exeter Book collection, but many of them are translated from or based on Latin originals; for example *Riddle 35*, Coat of Mail, translates Aldhelm's *De Lorica*.

On *Riddle 60*, see discussion of *Husband's Message* above p. 76.

BIBLIOGRAPHY

A. J. Wyatt, *Old English Riddles*, Boston, 1912
ASPR III
Sweet ASR contains nos. 7, 9, 14, 26, 47
Kershaw contains no. 60
C. L. Wrenn, *Studies in Old English Literature*, London, 1967, pp. 170–5

Riddles

5

Ic eom ānhaga,⠀⠀⠀īserne wund,
bille gebennad,⠀⠀⠀beadoweorca sæd,
ecgum wērig.⠀⠀⠀Oft ic wīg sēo,
frēcne feohtan;⠀⠀⠀frōfre ne wēne,
5⠀þæt mē gēoc cyme⠀⠀⠀gūðgewinnes,
ǣr ic mid ældum⠀⠀⠀eal forwurde;
ac mec hnossiað⠀⠀⠀homera lāfe,
heardecg, heoroscearp,⠀⠀⠀hondweorc smiþa
bītað in burgum;⠀⠀⠀ic ā bīdan sceal
10⠀lāþran gemōtes.⠀⠀⠀Nǣfre lǣcecynn
on folcstede⠀⠀⠀findan meahte
þāra þe mid wyrtum⠀⠀⠀wunde gehǣlde;
ac mē ecga dolg⠀⠀⠀ēacen weorðað
þurh dēaðslege⠀⠀⠀dagum and nihtum.

5. Shield.

7

Hrægl mīn swīgað⠀⠀⠀þonne ic hrūsan trede
oþþe þā wīc būge⠀⠀⠀oþþe wado drēfe.
Hwīlum mec āhebbað⠀⠀⠀ofer hæleþa byht
hyrste mīne⠀⠀⠀and þēos hēa lyft,
5⠀and mec þonne wīde⠀⠀⠀wolcna strengu
ofer folc byreð;⠀⠀⠀frætwe mīne
swōgað hlūde⠀⠀⠀and swinsiað,
torhte singað,⠀⠀⠀þonne ic getenge ne bēom
flōde and foldan,⠀⠀⠀fērende gǣst.

7. Swan.

96

Riddles

5

I am a lonely being, scarred by swords,
Wounded by iron, sated with battle-deeds,
Wearied by blades. Often I witness war,
Perilous fight, nor hope for consolation,
That any help may rescue me from strife
Before I perish among fighting men;
But hammered swords, hard edged and grimly sharp,
Batter me, and the handwork of the smith
Bites in the castles; I must ever wait
A contest yet more cruel. I could never
In any habitation find the sort
Of doctor who could heal my wounds with herbs;
But cuts from swords ever increase on me
Through deadly contest, both by day and night.

7

My dress is silent when I tread the ground
Or stay at home or stir upon the waters.
Sometimes my trappings and the lofty air
Raise me above the dwelling-place of men,
And then the power of clouds carries me far
Above the people; and my ornaments
Loudly resound, send forth a melody
And clearly sing, when I am not in touch
With earth or water, but a flying spirit.

9

Mec on þissum dagum   dēadne ofgēafun
fæder and mōdor;   ne wæs mē feorh þā gēn,
ealdor in innan.   Þā mec ān ongon
wel hold mēge,   wēdum þeccan,
5 hēold and freoþode,   hlēosceorpe wrāh
swā ārlīce   swā hire āgen bearn,
oþþæt ic under scēate,   swā mīn gesceapu wǣron,
ungesibbum wearð   ēacen gǣste.
Mec sēo friþemǣg   fēdde siþþan,
10 oþþæt ic āwēox,   wīddor meahte
sīþas āsettan;   hēo hæfde swǣsra þȳ lǣs
suna and dohtra   þȳ hēo swā dyde.

9. Cuckoo.
9.2. 'I had as yet no life', i.e. 'I was an egg.'

II

Hrægl is mīn hasofāg,   hyrste beorhte,
rēade and scīre   on rēafe mīnum.
Ic dysge dwelle   and dole hwette
unrǣdsīþas,   ōþrum stȳre
5 nyttre fōre.   Ic þæs nōwiht wāt
þæt hēo swā gemǣdde,   mōde bestolene,
dǣde gedwolene,   dēoraþ mīne
wōn wīsan gehwām.   Wā him þæs þēawes,
siþþan Hēah bringeð   horda dēorast,
10 gif hī unrǣdes   ǣr ne geswīcaþ.

11. Wine, though Night and Gold have been supported as the solution
by some editors. The problem centres upon the interpretation of l. 9.
Believers in Night take *horda deorast* to mean 'the sun', most others taking
it as 'the soul'. In the translation I follow Wyatt. See ASPR note.

9

Me in those days my father and my mother
Gave up as dead: I had as yet no life,
No spirit. Then a loyal kinswoman
Wrapped me in clothes and kept and cherished me,
Enfolded me in a protective cloak,
As kindly as she did for her own children,
Until, as was my nature, in her care
I became mighty-hearted among those
Who were no kin of mine. Yet my protectress
Still nourished me till I grew up and might
More widely travel. She by doing that
Had less dear sons and daughters of her own.

II

My dress is dark, but my adornments bright
And glittering and red among my clothing.
I lead astray the stupid, urge the fool
To rash adventures; others I restrain
From useful journeys. I have no idea
Why they, thus mad and having lost their minds,
Their deeds gone wrong, should glorify to all
My wicked ways. For this they shall have grief,
When the High Lord brings forth the dearest treasure,
If they have not then ceased in this bad counsel.

12

Fōtum ic fēre,   foldan slīte,
grēne wongas,   þenden ic gǣst bere.
Gif mē feorh losað,   fæste binde
swearte Wēalas,   hwīlum sēllan men.
5 Hwīlum ic dēorum   drincan selle
beorne of bōsme,   hwīlum mec brȳd triedeð
felawlonc fōtum,   hwīlum feorran brōht
wonfeax Wāle   wegeð and þȳð,
dol druncmennen   deorcum nihtum,
10 wǣteð in wætre,   wyrmeð hwīlum
fægre to fȳre;   mē on fæðme sticað
hygegālan hond,   hwyrfeð geneahhe,
swīfeð mē geond sweartne.   Saga hwæt ic hātte,
þe ic lifgende   lond rēafige
15 and æfter dēaþe   dryhtum þēowige.

12. Leather.

14

Ic wæs wǣpenwiga;   nū mec wlonc þeceð,
geong hagostealdmon   golde and sylfore,
wōum wīrbogum.   Hwīlum weras cyssað;
hwīlum ic tō hilde   hlēoþre bonne
5 wilgehlēþan;   hwīlum wycg byreþ
mec ofer mearce,   hwīlum merehengest
fereð ofer flōdas   frætwum beorhtne;
hwīlum mægða sum   mīnne gefylleð
bōsm bēaghroden;   hwīlum ic bordum sceal,
10 heard, hēafodlēas,   behlȳþed licgan;
hwīlum hongige   hyrstum frætwed,
wlitig on wāge,   þǣr weras drincað;
frēolic fyrdsceorp   hwīlum folcwigan
on wicge wegað;   þonne ic winde sceal

12

By foot I travel, and I tear the earth,
The grassy fields, as long as I have life.
But when my spirit leaves me I bind fast
The dark Welsh slaves or sometimes better men.
Sometimes I give a noble warrior
Drink from my breast; sometimes the haughty bride
Treads on me. Sometimes the dark-haired Welsh maid
Brought from afar carries and presses me,
A foolish drunken girl at dark of night
Wets me with water, sometimes pleasantly
Warms me beside the fire, sticks in my bosom
Her wanton hand, constantly turns me round,
Strokes me all night. Tell me what I am called,
That while I live may plunder all the land,
And after death give service to mankind.

14

I was a soldier armed; but now a proud
Young warrior covers me with gold and silver,
With twisted rings of wire. Sometimes men kiss me;
Sometimes by voice I summon to the battle
The loyal friends; sometimes a splendid steed
Bears me across the mark; sometimes a sea-horse
Gay in its colours ferries me across
The waters; or a maiden, ring-adorned,
Fills up my bosom; sometimes on the tables
I have to lie, hard, stripped, without my head;
Or sometimes beautiful, bedecked with trappings,
I hang upon the wall where heroes drink.
Sometimes when warriors wear their noble war-gear
On horseback, then must I, adorned with treasure,

15   sincfāg swelgan   of sumes bōsme;
      hwīlum ic gereordum   rincas laðige
      wlonce tō wīne;   hwīlum wrāþum sceal
      stefne mīnre   forstolen hreddan,
      flȳman fēondsceaþan.   Frige hwæt ic hātte.

14. Horn.
14.5. 'splendid' added in translation.

21

      Neb is mīn niþerweard;   nēol ic fēre
      and be grunde græfe,   geonge swā mē wīsað
      hār holtes fēond;   and hlāford mīn,
      se wōh færeð,   weard æt steorte
5   wrīgaþ on wonge,   wegeð mec and þȳð,
      sāweþ on swæð mīn.   Ic snyþige forð,
      brungen of bearwe,   bunden cræfte,
      wegen on wægne;   hæbbe wundra fela.
      Mē biþ gongendre   grēne on healfe,
10   and mīn swæð sweotol   sweart on ōþre.
      Mē þurh hrycg wrecen   hongaþ under
      ān orþonc pīl,   ōþer on hēafde
      fæst and forðweard.   Fealleþ on sīdan
      þæt ic tōþum tere,   gif mē teala þēnaþ
15   hindeweardre   þæt biþ hlāford mīn.

21. Plough.
21.3. *hār holtes feond* refers to the ploughman, as men chop down trees, or to the iron ploughshare, axes also being of iron.

26

      Mec fēonda sum   fēore besnyþede,
      woruldstrenga binōm,   wætte siþþan,
      dȳfde on wætre,   dyde eft þonan,
      sette on sunnan,   þǣr ic swīþe belēas
5   hērum þām þe ic hæfde.   Heard mec siþþan
      snāð seaxses ecg,   sindrum begrunden;

Swallow the wind puffed out from some man's breast;
Sometimes I summon by my proclamation
Proud men to wine; sometimes my voice must rescue
The stolen property from enemies,
Put foes to flight. Now find out what I am.

21

My beak points downwards, and I travel low
And dig along the ground, move forward as
The wood's old foe propels me; and my lord
And guardian walks stooping at my tail,
Pushes and moves and drives me on the field,
Sows in my track. I sniff along the ground,
Brought from the forest, firmly bound, and borne
Upon the wagon; I have many wonders.
And as I move on one side there is green
And my clear track is dark upon the other.
A well made point is driven through my back
And hangs beneath, and through my head another,
Firm, pointing forwards; what my teeth tear up
Falls down beside me, if he serves me well
Who, as my lord, controls me from behind.

26

Some enemy deprived me of my life
And took away my worldly strength, then wet me,
Dipped me in water, took me out again,
Set me in sunshine, where I quickly lost
The hairs I had. Later the knife's hard edge
Cut me with all impurities ground off.

fingras fēoldan,　　and mec fugles wyn
geond spēddropum　　spyrede geneahhe,
ofer brūnne brerd,　　bēamtelge swealg,
10　streames dǣle,　　stōp eft on mec,
sīþade sweartlāst.　　Mec siþþan wrāh
hæleð hlēobordum,　　hȳde beþenede,
gierede mec mid golde;　　forþon mē glīwedon
wrǣtlic weorc smiþa,　　wīre bifongen.
15　Nū þā gerēno　　and se rēada telg
and þā wuldorgesteald　　wīde mǣre
dryhtfolca Helm,　　nāles dol wīte.
Gif mīn bearn wera　　brūcan willað,
hȳ bēoð þȳ gesundran　　and þȳ sigefæstran,
20　heortum þȳ hwætran　　and þȳ hygeblīþran,
ferþe þȳ frōdran,　　habbaþ frēonda þȳ mā,
swǣsra and gesibbra,　　sōþra and gōdra,
tilra and getrēowra,　　þā hyra tȳr and ēad
ēstum ȳcað　　and hȳ ārstafum
25　lissum bilecgað　　and hī lufan fæþmum
fæste clyppað.　　Frige hwæt ic hātte,
niþum to nytte.　　Nama mīn is mǣre,
hæleþum gifre　　and hālig sylf.

26. The Bible.

34

Ic wiht geseah　　in wera burgum,
sēo þæt feoh fēdeð.　　Hafað fela tōþa;
nebb biþ hyre æt nytte,　　niþerweard gongeð,
hīþeð holdlīce　　and tō hām tȳhð,
5　wǣþeð geond weallas,　　wyrte sēceð;
āa hēo þā findeð,　　þā þe fæst ne biþ;
lǣteð hīo þā wlitigan,　　wyrtum fæste,
stille stondan　　on staþolwonge,
beorhte blīcan,　　blōwan and grōwan.

34. Rake.

Then fingers folded me; the bird's fine raiment
Traced often over me with useful drops
Across my brown domain, swallowed the tree-dye
Mixed up with water, stepped on me again
Leaving dark tracks. The hero clothed me then
With boards to guard me, stretched hide over me,
Decked me with gold; and thus the splendid work
Of smiths, with wire bound round, embellished me.
Now my red dye and all my decorations,
My gorgeous trappings far and wide proclaim
The Lord of Hosts, not grief for foolish sins.
If sons of men will make good use of me,
By that they shall be sounder, more victorious,
Their hearts more bold, their minds more full of joy,
Their spirits wiser; they shall have more friends,
Dear ones and kinsmen, truer and more good,
More kind and faithful, who will add more glory
And happiness by favours, who will lay
Upon them kindnesses and benefits,
And clasp them fast in the embrace of love.
Say who I am, useful to men. My name
Is famous, good to men, and also sacred.

34

I saw a creature in the homes of men
Which feeds the cattle. It has many teeth.
Its beak is useful to it. It points downwards.
It plunders gently and goes home again,
Wanders among the mounds and seeks out herbs.
It always finds out those that are not firm.
It lets the fair ones stand upon their roots,
Firm, undisturbed in their established place,
And brightly shine and blossom and grow tall.

47

Moððe word fræt.   Mē þæt þūhte
wrǣtlicu wyrd,   þā ic þæt wundor gefrægn,
þæt se wyrm forswealg   wera gied sumes,
þēof in þȳstro   þrymfæstne cwide
5 and þæs strangan staþol.   Stælgiest ne wæs
wihte þȳ glēawra,   þe hē þām wordum swealg.

47. Bookworm.
47.5. *stapol* 'foundation' refers to the parchment. The genitive *þæs strangan* is not easy to account for. Accusative *þone* for *þæs* would eliminate the problem.

60

Ic wæs be sonde,   sǣwealle nēah,
æt merefaroþe,   mīnum gewunade
frumstaþole fæst;   fēa ǣnig wæs
monna cynnes,   þæt mīnne þǣr
5 on ānǣde   eard behēolde,
ac mec ūhtna gehwām   ȳð sīo brūne
lagufæðme beleolc.   Lȳt ic wēnde
þæt ic ǣr oþþe sīð   ǣfre sceolde
ofer meodubence   mūðlēas sprecan,
10 wordum wrixlan.   Þæt is wundres dǣl,
on sefan searolic   þām þe swylc ne conn,
hū mec seaxes ord   and sēo swīþre hond,
eorles ingeþonc   and ord somod,
þingum geþȳdan,   þæt ic wiþ þē sceolde
15 for unc ānum twām   ǣrendsprǣce
ābēodan bealdlīce,   swā hit beorna mā
uncre wordcwidas   wīddor ne mǣnden.

60. Reed. See the prefatory remarks to *Husband's Message*, p. 76.

47

A moth ate words; a marvellous event
I thought it when I heard about that wonder,
A worm had swallowed some man's lay, a thief
In darkness had consumed the mighty saying
With its foundation firm. The thief was not
One whit the wiser when he ate those words.

60

Once I was at the sea-shore, by the sand,
Near the sea-wall I lived established firm
Upon my roots; and there were very few
Of humankind who looked upon my home
There in that lone and solitary land;
But every day the dark wave played with me
In watery embrace. I little thought
That late or early I at any time
Should ever mouthless speak across the mead-bench,
Communicate with words. It is a wonder
Amazing to the minds of those who know not
How the knife's point within the strong right hand,
The man's skill and the point worked busily
On me, so that I fearlessly could tell
A message to you, for the two of us
Alone to hear, so that no other man
Could hear and tell abroad our speech more widely.

Gnomic Verses

There are two OE sets of *Gnomic Verses*, of which I give the shorter. Their subject matter is a mixture of proverbial, preceptual and descriptive material. This type of work is probably very ancient, and these collections are in some respects similar to parts of the Old Norse *Hávamál*. However the Christian nature of these sets is beyond dispute, and indeed part of the other collection reads: 'Woden made idols, the Lord made heaven.' The Anglo-Saxon love of preceptual passages is evident from passages in *Wanderer*, *Deor*, and *Beowulf*, among others.

BIBLIOGRAPHY

ASPR VI, where they are called *Maxims II*
Sweet ASR

Gnomic Verses

Cyning sceal rīce healdan.   Ceastra bēoð feorran gesȳne,
orðanc enta geweorc,   þā þe on þysse eorðan syndon,
wrǣtlic weallstāna geweorc.   Wind byð on lyfte swiftust,
þunar byð þrāgum hlūdast.   Þrymmas syndan Crīsᵗes
myccle.
5 Wyrd byð swīðost.   Winter byð cealdost,
lencten hrīmigost,   hē byð lengest ceald,
sumor sunwlitegost,   swegel byð hātost,
hærfest hrēðēadegost,   hæleðum bringeð
gēres wæstmas   þā þe him God sendeð.
10 Sōð bið swutolost.   Sinc byð dēorost,
gold gumena gehwām,   and gomol snoterost,
fyrngēarum frōd,   se þe ǣr feala gebīdeð.
Wea bið wundrum clibbor.   Wolcnu scrīðað.
Geongne æþeling sceolan   gōde gesīðas
15 byldan tō beaduwe   and tō bēahgife.
Ellen sceal on eorle.   Ecg sceal wið helme
hilde gebīdan.   Hafuc sceal on glōfe
wilde gewunian;   wulf sceal on bearowe,
earm ānhaga;   eofor sceal on holte,
20 tōðmægenes trum.   Til sceal on ēðle
dōmes wyrcean.   Daroð sceal on handa,
gār golde fāh.   Gim sceal on hringe
standan stēap and gēap.   Strēam sceal on ȳðum
mencgan mereflōde.   Mæst sceal on cēole,
25 segelgyrd seomian.   Sweord sceal on bearme,
drihtlic īsern.   Draca sceal on hlǣwe,
frōd, frætwum wlanc.   Fisc sceal on wætere
cynren cennan.   Cyning sceal on healle
bēagas dǣlan.   Bera sceal on hǣðe,

2. *enta geweorc.* See note on *Ruin* l. 2. The second half-line, which appears
to say little, is probably to stress the earthly as opposed to heavenly nature
of much of the description in the poem. See note to *Epilogue to the Pastoral
Care* l. 6 and the last four lines of this poem.

Gnomic Verses

King shall rule kingdom. Cities from afar
Are seen, the skilful works of giants, those
Which are on this earth, splendid works of wall-stones.
Wind in the sky is fastest, thunder is
Loudest at times. The powers of Christ are great.
Fate is the mightiest; winter is the coldest,
Spring the most frosty, it is longest cold,
Summer most bright with sun, the heavens hottest,
Autumn most bountiful, it brings to men
The year's fruits which the Lord God sends to them.
Truth is most evident, treasure most precious,
Gold to each man; the aged are most wise,
Taught by past years, of much experience.
Grief clings remarkably. The welkin moves.
Noble companions must urge on the prince
While young to battle and to treasure-giving.
Warrior must be valiant; blade must strive
With helmet in the battle; the wild hawk
Must sit on glove; the wolf must live in wood
Wretched and lonely; boar must dwell in grove
Strong with his mighty tusks; the good on earth
Must work for glory; dart shall be in hand,
The gold-stained spear; jewel must stand on ring
Both high and broad; the stream must in the waves
Mix with the sea-flood; mast must be on ship,
The sail-yard tower; sword must be on breast,
The noble steel; dragon must live in mound,
Old, proud in his adornments; fish in water
Must propagate their race; the king in hall
Must share out rings; the old and fearsome bear

30   eald and egesfull.   Ēa of dūne sceal
      flōdgrǣg fēran.   Fyrd sceal ætsomne,
      tīrfæstra getrum.   Trēow sceal on eorle,
      wīsdōm on were.   Wudu sceal on foldan
      blǣdum blōwan.   Beorh sceal on eorþan
35   grēne standan.   God sceal on heofenum,
      dǣda Dēmend.   Duru sceal on healle,
      rūm recedes mūð.   Rand sceal on scylde,
      fæst fingra gebeorh.   Fugel uppe sceal
      lācan on lyfte.   Lcax sceal on wǣle
40   mid scēote scrīðan.   Scūr sceal of heofenum
      winde geblanden   in þās woruld cuman.
      Þēof sceal gangan þȳstrum wederum.   Þyrs sceal on
                                      fenne gewunian
      āna innan lande.   Ides sceal dyrne cræfte,
      fǣmne hire frēond gesēcean,   gif hēo nelle on folce
                                             geþēon,
45   þæt hī man bēagum gebicge.   Brim sceal sealte weallan,
      lyfthelm and laguflōd   ymb ealra landa gehwylc
      flōwan firgenstrēamas.   Feoh sceal on eorðan
      tȳdran and tȳman.   Tungol sceal on heofenum
      beorhte scīnan,   swā him bebēad Meotud.
50   Gōd sceal wið yfele;   geogoð sceal wið yldo;
      līf sceal wið dēaþe;   lēoht sceal wið þȳstrum;
      fyrd wið fyrde,   fēond wið ōðrum,
      lāð wið lāþe   ymb land sacan,
      synne stǣlan.   Ā sceal snotor hycgean
55   ymb þysse worulde gewinn;   wearh hangian,
      fǣgere ongildan   þæt hē ǣr fācen dyde
      manna cynne.   Meotod āna wāt
      hwyder sēo sāwul sceal   syððan hweorfan,
      and ealle þā gāstas   þe for Gode hweorfað

43-5. These lines are obscure. The buying with rings possibly refers to marriage.

Shall haunt the heath; the waters from the downs
Must flow, flood-grey; the troop must stick together,
The glorious band. Good faith must be in man,
Wisdom in warrior; wood must on the earth
Bloom with its fruits; the hill must stand out green
Above the land; God, Judge of deeds, shall dwell
In heaven. On the hall shall be a door,
The wide mouth of the house; shield must have boss,
Firm finger-guard; the birds up in the air
Shall play; and in the pool shall salmon sport
With trout; the shower falling from the sky
Stirred up by wind shall come into this world.
The thief shall work in dusky weather. Monster
Shall live alone on land among the fen.
Maiden by secret stealth must visit lover
Unless she wishes it to come about
Among the folk that she be bought with rings.
The sea shall surge with salt; cloud and sea-flood
Shall flow round every land in mighty streams.
Cattle shall breed and multiply on earth.
Stars shall shine brightly forth among the heavens
Just as the Lord commanded them to do.
Good against evil, youth shall strive with age,
Life against death, and light against the dark,
Army with army, foe against another,
Enemy fight with enemy for land,
Find cause for crime. Ever the prudent man
Must think about the fighting in this world;
Felon must hang, and justly pay the price
Because he first did crime against mankind.
Only God knows whither the soul shall go,
And all the spirits which shall turn to God

60 æfter dēaðdæge,   dōmes bīdað
   on Fæder fæðme.   Is sēo forðgesceaft
   dīgol and dyrne;   Drihten āna wāt,
   nergende Fæder.   Nǣni eft cymeð
   hider under hrōfas   þe þæt hēr for sōð
65 mannum secge   hwylc sȳ Meotodes gesceaft,
   sigefolca gesetu,   þǣr Hē sylfa wunað.

After the day of death and wait for judgment
In God's embrace. What is ordained to come
Is dark and secret, only known to God
The saving Father. None comes back again
To these abodes who here may truly tell
To men what the Lord God's decree may be,
The home of the victorious, where He lives.

A Charm

Eleven Anglo-Saxon Charms survive which contain passages of verse. The supernatural beliefs behind the rituals involved are in some clearly pre-Christian, while in others Christian ideas have been introduced, yet others being wholly Christian. Only in one is a pagan deity actually invoked, in a charm for unfruitful land, where after *inter alia* reference to St. Mary, the verses call upon 'Erce, Erce, Erce, mother of earth'. About Erce however nothing is known from other sources.

BIBLIOGRAPHY

ASPR VI

A Charm

Wenne, wenne,   wenchichenne,
hēr ne scealt þū timbrien,   ne nēnne tūn habben,
ac þū scealt north eonene   tō þān nīhgan berhge,
þēr þū hauest, ermig,   ēnne brōþer.
5 Hē þē sceal legge   lēaf et hēafde.
Under fōt wolues,   under uêþer earnes,
under earnes clēa,   ā þū geweornie.
Clinge þū   alswā cōl on heorþe,
scring þū   alswā scerne awāge,
10 and weorne   alswā weter on anbre.
Swā lītel þū gewurþe   alswā līnsētcorn,
and miccli lēsse alswā ānes handwurmes hupebān, and
alswā lītel þū gewurþe þet þū nāwiht gewurþe.

A Charm

O wen, wen, O little wennikins,
Here shall you build not, here have no abode,
But you must northwards to the nearby hill,
For there, O wretched one, you have a brother,
And he shall lay a leaf upon your head.
Under wolf's foot and under eagle's wing,
'Neath claw of eagle ever may you fade.
May you decrease like coal upon the hearth,
Shrivel away like dirt upon the wall,
Evaporate like water in a pail,
Become as little as a linseed-grain,
Much smaller than a hand-worm's hip-bone is,
And so diminish that you come to nothing.

Cædmon's Hymn

Our knowledge of the poet Cædmon comes from Bede's *Historia Ecclesiastica*, Book IV, Chapter 22, where the story is told of how at the monastery of Whitby Cædmon, who had formerly been unable to sing, was inspired to do so in a dream in which he sang this Hymn. On awaking he made known his new gift and was taken before the Abbess Hild, who instructed him to become a monk. He did so, and composed many other poems on religious subjects, some of which are listed by Bede. Though some extant OE poems are on the same subjects as some of those in Bede's list, detailed analysis has revealed that most of them cannot be by Cædmon, and only this Hymn can safely be attributed to him. One of the implications of Bede's account is that Cædmon was the first to use OE verse for composing religious poems, though this is not universally accepted. *Cædmon's Hymn* can be roughly dated as Hild was abbess at Whitby from 657–80.

The text here given is from an early MS and is in a Northumbrian dialect, though many MSS are extant, some of them in West Saxon.

BIBLIOGRAPHY

H. Sweet, *The Oldest English Texts*, EETS O.S. 83, London, 1885

A. H. Smith, *Three Northumbrian Poems*, Methuen's Old English Library, London, 1933, reprinted 1968 with corrections

ASPR VI

Sweet ASR

Pope, 7 OE P

C. L. Wrenn, 'The Poetry of Cædmon', *Proceedings of the British Academy*, XXXII, 1946

L. Sherly-Price, *Bede, A History of the English Church and People*, Penguin Classics, Harmondsworth, 1955, pp. 245–8

Cædmon's Hymn

Nū scylun hergan   hefænrīcæs Uard,
Metudæs mæcti   end His mōdgidanc,
uerc Uuldurfadur,   suē Hē uundra gihuæs,
ēci Dryctin,   ōr āstelidæ.
5   Hē ǣrist scōp   ælda barnum
heben til hrōfe,   hāleg Scepen.
Thā middungeard   moncynnæs Uard,
ēci Dryctin,   æfter tīadæ
fīrum foldu,   Frēa allmectig.

3–4. Literally 'the works of the Father of glory, as He, eternal Lord, made the beginning of every wonder'.
7. 'eternal' added in translation.

Cædmon's Hymn

Now must we praise the Guardian of heaven,
The power and conception of the Lord,
And all His works, as He, eternal Lord,
Father of glory, started every wonder.
First He created heaven as a roof,
The holy Maker, for the sons of men.
Then the eternal Keeper of mankind
Furnished the earth below, the land for men,
Almighty God and everlasting Lord.

Bede's Death Song

This song is quoted in the *Epistola Cuthberti de obitu Bedae*, Cuthbert being apparently a cleric who knew Bede and who later became abbot of Wearmouth and Jarrow. It seems that Bede did compose it, though it has been argued that he was quoting. Bede died in 735.

The Song is here given in Northumbrian, the situation being as for *Cædmon's Hymn* above.

BIBLIOGRAPHY

Editions are given in the works listed above under *Cædmon's Hymn* except that it is not in Pope.

Almsgiving

I have selected this as an attractive example from a number of short religious poems, which include translations of The Lord's Prayer, The Gloria, etc., found in the Exeter Book and elsewhere.

BIBLIOGRAPHY

ASPR III

Bede's Death Song

Fore thēm nēidfærǣ   nǣnig uuiurthit
thoncsnotturra   than him tharf sīe
tō ymbhycggannæ,   ǣr his hiniongæ,
huæt his gāstæ   gōdæs æththa yflæs
5 æfter dēothdæge   dōemid uueorthæ.

Almsgiving

Wel bið þām eorle   þe him on innan hafað,
rēþehygdig wer,   rūme heortan;
þæt him biþ for worulde   weorðmynda mǣst,
ond for ūssum Dryhtne   dōma sēlast.
5 Efne swā hē mid wætre   þone weallendan
lēg ādwǣsce,   þæt hē leng ne mæg
blāc byrnende   burgum sceððan,
swā hē mid ælmessan   ealle tōscūfeð
synna wunde,   sāwla lācnað.

Bede's Death Song

Before the journey that awaits us all,
No man becomes so wise that he has not
Need to think out, before his going hence,
What judgment will be given to his soul
After his death, of evil or of good.

Almsgiving

Well shall it be for the just-minded man
Who has within himself a spacious heart;
That shall bring greatest honour in the world
And best of judgment for him from our Lord.
And just as he could quench the surging flame
With water, that it might no longer harm
The brightly burning city, even so
Does he by almsgiving cast right away
The wounds of sinfulness, and heal his soul.

The Metrical Preface and Epilogue to the Pastoral Care

As part of his plan to improve the education of the English, King Alfred translated four works from the Latin. These were: Gregory the Great's *Pastoral Care*, Orosius's *Universal History*, Boethius's *Consolation of Philosophy*, and part of St. Augustine's *Soliloquies*. The Boethius contains passages of verse, and it is generally accepted that Alfred wrote the English verse translations of these (edited by G. P. Krapp, ASPR V). There is no good reason to doubt that he also wrote the verse Preface and Epilogue of his own translation of the *Pastoral Care*. We learn from Asser's *Life of King Alfred* that he heard Old English poems with attention and often memorised them. Alfred died in 899.

BIBLIOGRAPHY

H. Sweet, *King Alfred's West-Saxon Version of Gregory's Pastoral Care*, EETS O.S. 45, 50, London, 1871, 2.

ASPR VI

The Metrical Preface to the Pastoral Care

Þis ærendgewrit   Āgustīnus
ofer sealtne sæ   sūðan brōhte
īegbūendum,   swā hit ǣr fore
ādihtode   Dryhtnes cempa,
5 Rōme pāpa.   Ryhtspell monig
Grēgōrius   glēawmōd gindwōd
ðurh sefan snyttro,   searoðonca hord.
Forðǣm hē monncynnes   mǣst gestrīende
rōdra Wearde,   Rōmwara betest,
10 monna mōdwelegost,   mǣrðum gefrǣgost.
Siððan mīn on englisc   Ælfred kyning
āwende worda gehwelc,   and mē his wrīterum
sende sūð and norð,   heht him swelcra mā
brengan bi ðǣre bisene,   ðæt hē his biscepum
15 sendan meahte,   forðǣm hī his sume ðorfton,
    ðā ðe lædensprǣce   lǣste cūðon.

The Metrical Epilogue to the Pastoral Care

Ðis is nū se wæterscipe   ðe ūs wereda God
tō frōfre gehēt   foldbūendum.
Hē cwæð ðæt Hē wolde   ðæt on worulde forð
of ðǣm innoðum   ā libbendu
5 wætru flēowen,   ðe wel on Hine
gelīfden under lyfte.   Is hit lȳtel twēo
ðæt ðæs wæterscipes   welsprynge is
on hefonrīce,   ðæt is hālig gǣst.
Ðonan hine hlōdan   hālge and gecorene.
10 Siððan hine gierdon   ðā ðe Gode hērdon
ðurh hālga bēc   hider on eorðan
geond manna mōd   missenlīce.
Sume hine weriað   on gewitlocan,
wīsdōmes strēam,   welerum gehæftað,

The Metrical Preface to the Pastoral Care

Augustine brought this message from the south,
Over the salt sea to the island-dwellers,
As the Lord's general, the Pope of Rome,
Had earlier composed it. Wise in heart,
Gregory studied many sacred writings,
A hoard of learning, through his spirit's wisdom.
Thereby he most of all won over men
To heaven's Guardian, that best of Romans,
Of all mankind the richest in his spirit,
Most famous for his greatness. Afterwards
Alfred translated every word of me
Into the English tongue, and south and north
Despatched me to his scribes and ordered them
To make more copies from me, so that he
Could send them to his bishops, because some
Of them who knew least Latin needed it.

The Metrical Epilogue to the Pastoral Care

These are the waters which the Lord of Hosts
Promised as consolation to mankind.
He said it was His wish that evermore
Should living waters flow into the world
Out of the hearts of those who well believed
In Him beneath the sky. There can indeed
Be little doubt these waters have their spring
In heaven, that it is the Holy Ghost.
Thence it is drawn by saints and chosen men.
Then those who through the holy books have learnt
The joyful tidings spread them here on earth
Throughout the minds of men in diverse ways.
Some guard the stream of wisdom in their wits

15 ðæt hē on unnyt   ūt ne tōflōweð.
     Ac se wæl wunað   on weres brēostum
     ðurh Dryhtnes giefe   dīop and stille.
     Sume hine lǣtað   ofer landscare
     rīðum tōrinnan;   nis ðæt rǣdlic ðing,
20 gif swā hlūtor wæter,   hlūd and undīop,
     tōflōweð æfter feldum oð hit tō fenne werð.
     Ac hladað īow nū drincan,   nū īow Dryhten geaf
     ðæt īow Grēgōrius   gegiered hafað
     tō durum īowrum   Dryhtnes welle.
25 Fylle nū his fǣtels,   se ðe fæstne hider
     kylle brōhte,   cume eft hræðe.
     Gif hēr ðegna hwelc   ðȳrelne kylle
     brōhte tō ðȳs burnan,   bēte hine georne,
     ðȳ lǣs hē forscēade   scīrost wætra,
30 oððe him līfes drync   forloren weorðe.

6. *under lyfte*. This apparently meaningless tag had an important signifi-
cance for the medieval man, who had a very clear image of the universe
and who dwelt where within it. Mankind was well aware of the differences
between its own nature and surroundings and those of the angels and other
higher creatures, who all had their established geographical position. See
C. S. Lewis, *The Discarded Image*, Cambridge, 1964, especially Chapters V
and VII.

Locked up, and hold it captive by their lips,
That it may not flow uselessly away.
But yet the spring remains in that man's breast
Deep and still through the giving of the Lord.
Some let it run forth over all the land
In streams; but it is not advisable
That such clear water flow across the fields
Shallow and loud till it becomes a marsh.
But draw you now to drink, now God has granted
That Gregory has thus prepared for you
The well of God beside your very door.
Let him who here has quickly brought his jug
Fill now his vessel, then come back for more.
If any servant to this spring has brought
A leaking jug, let him in haste repair it,
Lest he should pour away that clearest water,
Or lest the drink of life be lost to him.

Judith

I choose this as a sufficiently short and particularly attractive piece to represent the poems based on biblical narrative. It is found in the same MS as *Beowulf*, but part of the poem is missing, though how much is uncertain. It does not slavishly follow its original, but has been converted into a highly skilful piece of narrative, with lingering attention to the salient points of the action, ingenious but relevant passages of interspersed moral comment, and trenchant and dramatic speeches. As usual in Old English there is no attempt at suspense (see ll. 9, 63, etc.). The whole poem is direct, bold and vivid, and it is the skill of the poet that makes it so despite his strong dependence on conventions and formulas; compare ll. 209–12 with *The Battle of Maldon* ll. 106–7, *The Battle of Brunanburh* ll. 60–5.

BIBLIOGRAPHY

B. J. Timmer, *Judith*, Methuen's Old English Library, London, 1952
ASPR IV
Sweet ASR

Judith

...... twēode
gifena in ðȳs ginnan grunde;   hēo ðǣr þā gearwe funde
mundbyrd æt ðām mǣran Þēodne,   þā hēo āhte mǣste
                    þearfe
hyldo þæs hēhstan Dēman,   þæt hē hīe wið þæs hēhstan
                    brōgan
5 gefriðode, frymða Waldend;   hyre ðæs Fæder on roderum
torhtmōd tīðe gefremede,   þe hēo āhte trumne gelēafan
ā tō ðām Ælmihtigan.   Gefrægen ic ðā Hōlofernus
wīnhātan wyrcean georne,   and eallum wundrum þrymlic
girwan up swǣsendo: tō ðām hēt se gumena baldor
10 ealle ðā yldestan ðegnas: hīe ðæt ofstum miclum
ræfndon rondwiggende,   cōmon tō ðām rīcan þēodne
fēran folces rǣswan.   Þæt wæs þȳ fēorðan dōgore
þæs ðe Iūdith hyne   glēaw on geðonce,
ides ælfscīnu,   ǣrest gesōhte.
15 Hīe ðā tō ðām symle   sittan ēodon,
wlance tō wīngedrince,   ealle his wēagesīðas,
bealde byrnwiggende.   Þǣr wǣron bollan stēape
boren æfter bencum gelōme,   swylce ēac būnan and orcas
fulle fletsittendum: hīe þæt fǣge þēgon
20 rōfe rondwiggende,   þēah ðæs se rīca ne wēnde,
egesful eorla dryhten.   Ðā wearð Hōlofernus,
goldwine gumena,   on gytesālum;
hlōh and hlȳdde,   hlynede and dynede,
þæt mihten fīra bearn   feorran gehȳran,
25 hū se stīðmōda   styrmde and gylede,
mōdig and medugāl   manode geneahhe
bencsittende   þæt hī gebǣrdon wel.
Swā se inwidda   ofer ealne dæg
dryhtguman sīne   drencte mid wīne,

1. The negative in the translation is deduced from the context.

Judith

... And did not doubt his gifts in this wide world.
She found there ready help from the great Prince
When most she needed from the Highest Judge
Favour, that He, the Ruler of creation,
Should save her from the greatest of all terrors.
The Father in the heavens, glorious,
Granted her plea, because she always had
Firm faith in the Almighty. Then I heard
That Holofernes summoned men to wine
And splendidly prepared a mighty banquet,
To which the prince of men commanded all
His noblest thanes. The soldiers with great speed
Did as he bade, the people's leaders came
To the great ruler. That was the fourth day
After the elf-fair lady Judith first,
Wise in her heart, had come to visit him.
They went and sat then at the feast, proud men
At wine-drinking, all his comrades in woe,
The bold armed warriors. There were steep bowls
Borne often round the benches, likewise cups
And tankards full to all who sat in hall.
The brave men who accepted it were doomed,
Though this the strong and dreadful lord of men
Did not foresee. Then Holofernes was
In festive mood, the patron of those men.
He laughed and roared, he shouted and cried out,
So that the sons of men could hear afar
How the stern-spirited one stormed and yelled,
Mead-drunk and proud continuously urged
Those on the benches to enjoy themselves.
And so the evil one throughout the day,
Arrogant patron, drenched his men with wine

30 swīðmōd sinces brytta,   oð þæt hīe on swīman lāgon,
   oferdrencte his duguðe ealle,   swylce hīe wæron dēaðe
                       geslegene,
   āgotene gōda gehwylces.   Swā hēt se gumena aldor
   fylgan fletsittendum,   oð þæt fīra bearnum
   nēalǣhte niht sēo þȳstre.   Hēt ðā nīða geblonden
35 þā ēadigan mægð   ofstum fetigan
   tō his bedreste   bēagum gehlæste,
   hringum gehrodene.   Hīe hraðe fremedon
   anbyhtsccalcas,   swā him hcora ealdor bebēad,
   byrnwigena brego: bearhtme stōpon
40 tō ðām gysterne,   þær hīe Iūdithðe
   fundon ferhðglēawe,   and ðā fromlīce
   lindwiggende   lǣdan ongunnon
   þā torhtan mægð   tō træfe þām hēan,
   þær se rīca hyne   reste on symbel,
45 nihtes inne,   Nergende lāð
   Hōlofernus.   Þær wæs eallgylden
   flēohnet fæger   ymbe þæs folctogan
   bed āhongen,   þæt se bealofulla
   mihte wlītan þurh,   wigena baldor,
50 on æghwylcne   þe ðǣrinne cōm
   hæleða bearna,   and on hyne nǣnig
   monna cynnes,   nymðe se mōdiga hwæne
   nīðe rōfra   him þē nēar hēte
   rinca tō rūne gegangan.   Hīe ðā on reste gebrōhton
55 snūde ðā snoteran idese;   ēodon ðā stercedferhðe
   hæleð heora hearran cȳðan   þæt wæs sēo hālige mēowle
   gebrōht on his būrgetelde.   Þā wearð se brēma on mōde
   blīðe, burga ealdor,   þōhte ðā beorhtan idese
   mid wīdle and mid womme besmītan;   ne wolde þæt
                       wuldres Dēma
60 geðafian, þrymmes Hyrde,   ac hē him þæs ðinges
                       gestȳrde,
   Dryhten, dugeða Waldend.   Gewāt ðā se dēofulcunda,

61. *Dryhten* omitted in translation.

Till all his troop was drunk and lay unconscious
As if struck down in death, deprived of good.
Thus did the prince of warriors command
That those in hall be served, until dark night
Approached the sons of men. Then, steeped in sin,
He ordered that the blessed maid be fetched,
Laden with ornaments and decked with rings,
To grace his bed. Retainers quickly did
As their prince bade, the lord of war-armed men.
To the guest-house they noisily repaired,
And there wise-hearted Judith did they find;
The warriors at once began to lead
The noble maiden to the high pavillion
Where the great lord used always to retire,
The nightly chamber of Holofernes
The Saviour's foe. There was a curtain fair,
All-golden, hung around the leader's bed
So that the wicked lord could see through it
On any hero's son who came therein.
But none could look on him unless the chief
Should order any of the brave in war
To come more close to him for consultation.
Then they brought the wise lady to his couch
Speedily, and the steadfast men went out
To tell their prince the holy woman had
Been taken to his tent. The famous prince
Of cities then exulted in his heart,
Planned to pollute that lady fair with sin
And foulness; but the Guardian of might,
The Judge of glory would not let it be,
The King of hosts restrained him from the deed.
The fiendish one then with a troop of men,

gālferhð gangan   gumena ðrēate
bealofull his beddes nēosan,   þǣr hē sceolde his blǣd
                                     forlēosan
ǣdre binnan ānre nihte;   hæfde ðā his ende gebidenne
65 on eorðan unswǣslicne,   swylcne hē ǣr æfter worhte,
þearlmōd ðēoden gumena,   þenden hē on ðysse worulde
wunode under wolcna hrōfe.   Gefēol ðā wīne swā druncen
se rīca on his reste middan,   swā hē nyste rǣda nānne
on gewitlocan;   wiggend stōpon
70 ūt of ðām inne   ofstum miclum,
weras wīnsade,   þe ðone wǣrlogan,
lāðne lēodhatan,   lǣddon tō bedde
nēhstan sīðe.   Þā wæs Nergendes
þēowen þrymful   þearle gemyndig
75 hū hēo þone atolan   ēaðost mihte
ealdre benǣman   ǣr se unsȳfra,
womfull onwōce.   Genam ðā wundenlocc,
Scyppendes mægð,   scearpne mēce,
scūrum heardne,   and of scēaðe ābrǣd
80 swīðran folme;   ongan ðā swegles Weard
be naman nemnan,   Nergend ealra
woruldbūendra,   and þæt word ācwæð:
'Ic Ðē frymða God,   and frōfre Gǣst,
Bearn Alwaldan   biddan wylle

62. *gangan* supplied. However as this line is surrounded by hypermetric verses, Timmer, ASPR and others are probably right in regarding *galferhð gumena ðreate* as the first half-line with the second missing by accident or design (see note on *Battle of Maldon* l. 172).

74. *þearle* omitted in translation.

79. *scurum heardne. Beowulf* l. 1033 and *Andreas* l. 1133 have the word *scurheard. Beowulf* l. 326 has also *regnhearde*. The latter probably originally meant 'supernaturally hard', the first element being related to Norse *regin*, 'gods'. This became thought to be the same as *regn*, 'rain', with some such idea as 'raining with weapons' in mind (see *Judith* l. 221, *flana scuras*), and then the nearly synonymous *scur* could be substituted as alliteration demanded. See C. L. Wrenn, *Beowulf with the Finnesburg Fragment*, London, 1958, p. 81.

Lustful and evil, set off for his bed,
Where he was destined soon that very night
To forfeit all his fame. Then had he reached
A cruel end on earth, such as before
The mighty prince of men had merited,
While in this world he lived under the roof
Of heaven. On his bed the noble lord
Fell down, so drunk with wine that in his mind
He knew no sense. The soldiers with great haste
Marched from the room, the men replete with wine,
Who for the last time to his bed had brought
The treacherous and hateful tyrant king.
Then was the mighty hand-maid of the Saviour
Mindful of how she might most easily
Deprive the fearful sinner of his life
Before the foul, impure one should awake.
The maiden of the Lord, with braided hair,
Seized a sharp sword hardened by battle-play,
And with her right hand drew it from its sheath.
Then she began to call upon the Lord
Of heaven by His name and the Protector
Of all who dwell on earth, and said these words:
'To you, God of creation, joyous Spirit,
And Son of the Almighty, will I pray:

85 miltse Þīnre   mē þearfendre,
Ðrȳnesse ðrym.   Ðearle ys mē nū ðā
heorte onhǣted   and hige gēomor,
swȳðe mid sorgum gedrēfed;   forgif mē, swegles Ealdor,
sigor and sōðne gelēafan,   þæt ic mid þȳs sweorde mōte
90 gehēawan þysne morðres bryttan;   geunne me mīnra
                        gesynta,
þearlmōd Þēoden gumena: nāhte ic Þīnre nǣfre
miltse þon māran þearfe: gewrec nū, mihtig Dryhten,
torhtmōd tīres Brytta,   þæt mē ys þus torne on mōde,
hāte on hreðre mīnum.'   Hī ðā se hēhsta Dēma
95 ǣdre mid elne onbryrde,   swā Hē dēð ānra gehwylcne
hērbūendra   þe Hyne him tō helpe sēceð
mid rǣde and mid rihte gelēafan.   Þā wearð hyre rūme
                        on mōde,
Hāligre hyht genīwod;   genam ðā þone hǣðenan mannan
fæste be feaxe sīnum,   tēah hyne folmum wið hyre weard
100 bysmerlīce,   and þone bealofullan
listum ālēde,   lāðne mannan,
swā hēo ðæs unlǣdan   ēaðost mihte
wel gewealdan.   Slōh ðā wundenlocc
þone fēondsceaðan   fāgum mēce
105 heteþoncolne,   þæt hēo healfne forcearf
þone swēoran him,   þæt hē on swīman læg,
druncen and dolhwund.   Næs ðā dēad þā gȳt,
ealles orsāwle: slōh ðā eornoste
ides ellenrōf   ōþre sīðe
110 þone hǣðenan hund,   þæt him þæt hēafod wand
forð on ðā flōre;   læg se fūla lēap
gēsne beæftan,   gǣst ellor hwearf
under neowelne næs   and ðǣr genyðerad wæs,
sūsle gesǣled   syððan ǣfre,

96. The first half-line appears to be normal, the second hypermetric.
J. C. Pope, *The Rhythm of Beowulf*, p. 220, suggests there is a missing word,
and proposes *heanra herbuendra*.

Show me your mercy in my need, O Might
Of Trinity. For greatly is my heart
Inflamed, my mind is sad and bitterly
Oppressed with sorrows. Grant me, heaven's Prince,
A victory and true belief, that I
May cut down with this sword the murderer.
Grant me my safety, mighty Prince of men.
I never had more need of Your protection.
Avenge now, mighty Lord and glorious
Giver of fame, that I have in my heart
Such bitterness, such warmth within my breast.'
The Highest Judge inspired her speedily
With valour, as He does to every one
Who lives on earth and comes to Him for help
With counsel and true faith. Then was her heart
Relieved, hope in the Holy One renewed.
She took the heathen man fast by his hair,
Pulled him towards her shamefully by hand,
Skilfully placed the evil, hated wretch
As she might best have power over him.
The fair-tressed one then struck the hated foe
With decorated sword, so that she cut
Through half his neck, and he lay swooning there,
Drunken and wounded. He was not yet dead,
Utterly lifeless; then the gallant girl
Earnestly smote the heathen hound again,
So that his head rolled forth upon the floor.
The foul trunk lay there dead, the spirit passed
Elsewhere under the cliff of the abyss,
And, there brought low, was bound in pain for ever,

115 wyrmum bewunden,   wītum gebunden,
    hearde gehæfted   in hellebryne
    æfter hinsīðe.   Ne ðearf hē hopian nō,
    þȳstrum forðylmed,   þæt hē ðonan mōte
    of ðām wyrmsele,   ac ðǣr wunian sceal
120 āwa to aldre   būtan ende forð
    in ðām heolstran hām   hyhtwynna lēas.
    Hæfde ðā gefohten   foremǣrne blǣd
    Iūdith æt gūðe,   swā hyre God ūðe,
    swegles Ealdor,   þe hyre sigores onlēah.
125 Þā sēo snotere mægð   snūde gebrōhte
    þæs herewǣðan   hēafod swā blōdig
    on ðām fǣtelse   þe hyre foregenga,
    blāchlēor ides,   hyra bēgea nest
    ðēawum geðungen   þyder on lǣdde,
130 and hit ðā swā heolfrig   hyre on hond āgeaf,
    higeðoncolre   hām tō berenne,
    Iūdith gingran sīnre.   Ēodon ðā gegnum þanonne
    þā idesa bā   ellenþrīste,
    oð þæt hīe becōmon   collenferhðe,
135 ēadhrēðige mægð   ūt of ðām herige,
    þæt hīe sweotollīce   gesēon mihten
    þǣre wlitegan byrig   weallas blīcan,
    Bēthūliam.   Hīe ðā bēahhrodene
    fēðelāste   forð ōnettan,
140 oð hīe glædmōde   gegān hæfdon
    tō ðām wealgate.   Wiggend sǣton,
    weras wæccende   wearde hēoldon
    in ðām fæstenne,   swā ðām folce ǣr
    gēomormōdum   Iūdith bebēad,
145 searoðoncol mægð,   þā hēo on sīð gewāt,
    ides ellenrōf.   Wæs ðā eft cumen
    lēof tō lēodum,   and ðā lungre hēt
    glēawhȳdig wīf   gumena sumne

117. *hinsiðe*, i.e. from this world. See note to *Epilogue to the Pastoral Care* l. 6.

Circled by serpents, fixed in punishments,
Held hard as captive in the burning hell
After his journey hence. He need not hope,
Wrapped round with darkness, that he may escape
Thence from the serpent-hall, but there must dwell
To all eternity in that dark home
Lacking all hope of bliss for evermore.
Then in the fight had Judith won herself
Outstanding glory, as God granted her
When heaven's Prince gave her the victory.
The wise maid quickly put the warrior's head,
All bloody as it was, into the bag
Which her fair-faced attendant girl had brought,
Most excellent in virtues, with their food,
And gave it back, thus gory, to her hand,
To carry home, Judith to her wise servant.
The valiant ladies both departed thence
At once, till triumphing the bold maids came
Out of that host, till they could clearly see
The walls of the fair city shining out,
Of Bethulia. Then, adorned with rings,
They hastened on their way till glad in heart
They reached the city wall. There soldiers sat,
And wakeful warriors in the fort kept watch,
As Judith, noble lady, prudent maid,
Had ordered the sad people earlier
When she set out. Was then come back again
The dear one to her people. The wise maid
Ordered one of the warriors at once

of ðǣre ginnan byrig   hyre tōgēanes gān,
150 and hī ofostlīce   in forlǣton
    þurh ðæs wealles geat,   and þæt word ācwæð
    tō ðām sigefolce: 'Ic ēow secgan mæg
    þoncwyrðe þing,   þæt gē ne þyrfen leng
    murnan on mōde: ēow ys Metod blīðe,
155 cyninga Wuldor;   þæt gecȳðed wearð
    geond woruld wīde,   þæt ēow ys wuldorblǣd
    torhtlic tōweard   and tīr gifeðe
    þāra lǣðða   þe gē lange drugon.'
    Þā wurdon blīðe   burhsittende,
160 syððan hī gehȳrdon   hū sēo hālige spræc
    ofer hēanne weall.   Here wæs on lustum,
    wið þæs fæstengeates   folc ōnette,
    weras wīf somod,   wornum and hēapum,
    ðrēatum and ðrymmum   þrungon and urnon
165 ongēan ðā Þēodnes mægð   þūsendmǣlum,
    ealde ge geonge: ǣghwylcum wearð
    men on ðǣre medobyrig   mōd ārēted,
    syððan hīe ongēaton   þæt wæs Iūdith cumen
    eft tō ēðle,   and ðā ofostlīce
170 hīe mid ēaðmēdum   in forlēton.
    Þā sēo glēawe hēt   golde gefrætewod
    hyre ðīnenne   þancolmōde
    þæs herewǣðan   hēafod onwrīðan,
    and hyt tō bēhðe   blōdig ætȳwan
175 þām burhlēodum,   hū hyre æt beaduwe gespēow.
    Spræc ðā sēo æðele   tō eallum þām folce:
    'Hēr gē magon sweotole,   sigerōfe hæleð,
    lēoda rǣswan,   on ðæs lāðestan
    hǣðenes heaðorinces   hēafod starian,
180 Hōlofernus   unlyfigendes,
    þe ūs monna mǣst   morðra gefremede,
    sārra sorga,   and þæt swȳðor gȳt
    ȳcan wolde;   ac him ne ūðe God
    lengran līfes,   þæt hē mid lǣððum ūs

To go and meet her from the spacious city
And quickly let them pass in through the gate,
And spoke these words to the victorious people:
'I tell you a most memorable thing,
That you need mourn no longer in your hearts.
The glorious Lord of kings is good to you.
It has been widely shown throughout the world
That splendid and magnificent renown
Is granted you, and glory shall be yours
From the afflictions you have long endured.'
Then were the dwellers in the city glad,
When they heard how the holy maiden spoke
Over the lofty wall. The host rejoiced,
The people hastened to the castle gate,
Women and men together, groups and troops,
In crowds and multitudes they thronged and ran
To meet the Prince's maiden in their thousands,
Both old and young; the heart of every man
Was gladdened in the celebrating city,
After they knew that Judith had returned
Back to her country, and then hastily
With humble reverence they let her in.
Then the wise lady, all adorned with gold,
Ordered her prudent maidservant to show
The warrior's head, unwrap it bloody there,
A token for the citizens to see
How she had prospered in the battle-play.
The noble one then spoke to all the people:
'There you may clearly gaze, triumphant heroes,
Leaders of warriors, upon the head
Of the most hateful heathen general,
Of the no longer living Holofernes,
Who most of all brought violence upon us
And bitter grief, and that more greatly still
Wished to increase; but God did not allow
Him longer life, that he with persecution

185 eglan mōste: ic him ealdor oðþrong
    þurh Godes fultum.   Nū ic gumena gehwæne
    þyssa burglēoda   biddan wylle,
    randwiggendra,   þæt gē recene ēow
    fȳsan tō gefeohte;   syððan frymða God,
190 ārfæst Cyning,   ēastan sende
    lēohtne lēoman,   berað linde forð,
    bord for brēostum   and byrnhomas,
    scīre helmas   in sceaðena gemong,
    fyllan folctogan   fāgum sweordum,
195 fæge frumgāras.   Fȳnd syndon ēowere
    gedēmed tō dēaðe   and gē dōm āgon,
    tīr æt tohtan,   swā ēow getācnod hafað
    mihtig Dryhten   þurh mīne hand.'
    Þā wearð snelra werod   snūde gegearewod,
200 cēnra tō campe;   stōpon cynerōfe
    secgas and gesīðas,   bæron sigeþūfas,
    fōron tō gefeohte   forð on gerihte,
    hæleð under helmum   of ðære hāligan byrig
    on ðæt dægred sylf;   dynedan scildas,
205 hlūde hlummon.   Þæs se hlanca gefeah
    wulf in walde,   and se wanna hrefn,
    wælgīfre fugel: wiston bēgen
    þæt him ðā þēodguman   þōhton tilian
    fylle on fǣgum;   ac him flēah on lāst
210 earn ǣtes georn,   ūrigfeðera,
    salowigpāda   sang hildelēoð,
    hyrnednebba.   Stōpon heaðorincas,
    beornas tō beadowe   bordum beðeahte,
    hwealfum lindum,   þā ðe hwīle ǣr
215 eldēodigra   edwīt þoledon,
    hǣðenra hosp;   him þæt hearde wearð
    æt ðām æscplegan   eallum forgolden
    Assȳrium,   syððan Ebrēas
    under gūðfanum   gegān hæfdon
220 tō ðām fyrdwīcum.   Hīe ðā fromlice

Might harm us; I deprived him of his life
With God's assistance. Now I wish to pray
To every man among the citizens
And warriors, that you prepare yourselves
Quickly for fight, after the gracious King,
Creator God, shall send forth from the east
The beams of light. Then bear forth linden-shields
Before your breasts, and ring-mailed corslets too,
And gleaming helmets in the press of foes,
Cut down their officers with flashing swords,
Their fated leaders. For your enemies
Are doomed to death, and you shall have renown,
Glory in battle, as the mighty God
Has shown you by this token through my hand.'
Quickly the troop of bold and eager men
Prepared themselves for fight. Then they advanced,
Brave warriors and comrades, bearing banners,
The heroes in their helmets straight away
Set off for battle from the holy city
At break of day itself. The shields resounded,
Loudly rang out. The lean wolf in the wood
Rejoiced at this, and the dark raven too,
The slaughter-greedy bird; for they both knew
That warriors intended to supply them
With doomed men for a feast. Behind them flew
The eagle keen for carnage, dewy-winged,
With feathers dark; the horny-beaked one sang
A song of battle. Warriors advanced,
Soldiers to war protected by their shields,
Their hollow boards, men who till then had long
Endured the shameful pride of foreigners,
The scorn of heathens. The Assyrians
Were all most grievously repaid for that
At the spear-play, after the Hebrew men
Under their warlike banners had approached
Their camping-place. They rapidly made showers

lēton forð flēogan   flāna scūras,
hildenǣdran   of hornbogan,
strǣlas stedehearde;   styrmdon hlūde
grame gūðfrecan,   gāras sendon
225 in heardra gemang;   hæleð wǣron yrre,
landbūende   lāðum cynne,
stōpon styrnmōde,   stercedferhðe
wrehton unsōfte   ealdgenīðlan
medowērige,   mundum brugdon
230 scealcas of scēaðum   scĪrmǣled swyrd
ecgum gecoste,   slōgon eornoste
Assīria   ōretmæcgas,
nīðhycgende,   nānne ne sparedon
þæs herefolces   hēanne ne rīcne
235 cwicera manna   þe hīe ofercuman mihton.
    Swā ðā magoþegnas   on ðā morgentīd
ēhton elðēoda   ealle þrāge,
oð þæt ongēaton   ðā ðe grame wǣron,
ðæs herefolces   hēafodweardas,
240 þæt him swyrdgeswing   swīðlic ēowdon
weras Ebrisce.   Hīe wordum þæt
þām yldestan   ealdorþegnum
cȳðan ēodon,   wrehton cumbolwigan
and him forhtlīce   fǣrspel bodedon,
245 medowērigum   morgencollan,
atolne ecgplegan.   Þā ic ǣdre gefrægn
slegefǣge hæleð   slǣpe tōbrēdon
and wið þæs bealofullan   būrgeteldes
wērigferhðe   hwearfum þringan
250 Hōlofernus;   hogedon āninga
hyra hlāforde   hilde bodian,
ǣr ðon ðe him se egesa   on ufan sǣte,
mægen Ebrēa.   Mynton ealle
þæt se beorna brego   and sēo beorhte mægð

---

223. *stedehearde*, found only here, has defied precise interpretation. See ASPR note on pp. 285–6.

Of darts fly forth, and from their horn-shaped bows
Sent battle-adders, strong and steady arrows.
Loudly they raged, the angry fighting men,
And sent their spears into the throng of fierce ones.
The heroes were enraged, the native people
Against the nation of their enemies.
Stern-hearted they advanced, and firm in spirit
They woke ungently their old enemies
Drunken with mead. By hand the warriors
Drew from the sheathes the ornate gleaming swords
With peerless edges, and struck earnestly
The warriors of the Assyrians,
The cruel-hearted ones; none did they spare
In all that army, neither low nor high,
No living man that they could overcome.
So the retainers in the morning-time
Pursued the foreigners unceasingly
Until the leaders of the hostile force,
Those who were hardy, clearly understood
That there the Hebrews made their sword-swing felt
Firmly upon them. Then they went and told
The seniors among the chief retainers,
Woke up the standard-bearers fearfully,
And told them, drunk with mead, the sudden news,
The morning terror and the sword-play grim.
Then, as I heard, the heroes doomed to slaughter
Quickly cast sleep aside and thronged in crowds,
Men grieving in their hearts, towards the tent
Of evil Holofernes, for they planned
To tell their lord at once about the fight
Before the terror of the Hebrew strength
Should set upon them. They remembered all
That the men's leader and the lovely maid

255 in ðām wlitegan træfe   wæron ætsomne,
Iūdith sēo æðele   and se gālmōda,
egesfull and āfor;   næs ðēah eorla nān,
þe ðone wiggend   āweccan dorste
oððe gecunnian   hū ðone cumbolwigan
260 wið ðā hālgan mægð   hæfde geworden,
Metodes mēowlan.   Mægen nēalǣhte,
folc Ebrēa,   fuhton þearle
heardum heoruwǣpnum,   hǣste guldon
hyra fyrngeflitu   fāgum swyrdum
265 ealde æfðoncan;   Assȳria wearð
on ðām dægweorce   dōm geswiðrod,
bælc forbīged.   Beornas stōdon
ymbe hyra þēodnes træf   þearle gebylde,
sweorcendferhðe.   Hī ðā somod ealle
270 ongunnon cohhettan,   cirman hlūde,
and grīstbitian   gode orfeorme,
mid tōðon torn þoligende;   þā wæs hyra tīres æt ende,
ēades and ellendǣda.   Hogedon þā eorlas āweccan
hira winedryhten: him wiht ne spēow.
275 Þā wearð sīð and late   sum tō ðām arod
þāra beadorinca,   þæt hē in þæt būrgeteld
nīðheard nēðde,   swā hyne nȳd fordrāf:
funde ðā on bedde   blācne licgan,
his goldgifan   gǣstes gēsne,
280 līfes belidenne.   Hē þā lungre gefēoll
frēorig tō foldan,   ongan his feax teran,
hrēoh on mōde,   and his hrægl somod,
and þæt word ācwæð   tō ðām wiggendum,
þe ðǣr unrōte   ūte wǣron:
285 'Hēr ys geswutelod   ūre sylfra forwyrd,
tōweard getācnod,   þæt þǣre tīde ys

287–8. *nu* and *life* supplied. Some editors expand the remaining words into one hypermetric line instead of two normal lines, placing *somod* at the beginning of the next (my l. 289). There is much to be said for this, as the second half-line of l. 289 appears to be hypermetric.

Were both together in the splendid tent,
The noble Judith and the lustful one,
Fearsome and harsh. But there was no-one there
Among the warriors who durst awake
The general, or would investigate
How the great leader with the holy maid
Had prospered, with the woman of the Lord.
The force approached, the army of the Hebrews
Fought vigorously with their hardy weapons,
Firmly repaid their former suffering
And long-held grudge with decorated swords.
The glory of Assyria declined
By that day's work, and brought down was their pride.
The warriors stood round their prince's tent
Gravely disturbed, with spirits darkening.
They then together all began to cough,
To cry out loudly and to gnash their teeth,
Deprived of joy and suffering great grief.
Then were success, glory and noble deeds
Ended for them. The warriors designed
To wake their lord; but it availed them not.
But then at last one of the warriors
Grew bold enough, and daring ventured in
To the pavillion, as compulsion drove.
And there he found his patron lying pale
Upon his couch, deprived of consciousness,
Departed from this life. At once he fell
Cold to the ground, began to tear his hair
And clothing likewise, in his heart enraged,
And called these words out to the warriors
Who waited gloomily outside for him:
'Here is our own destruction shown to us,
Its coming tokened, that the time is near

nū mid nīðum   nēah geðrungen,
þe wē līfe sculon   losian somod,
æt sæcce forweorðan: hēr līð sweorde gehēawen,
290 behēafdod healdend ūre.'   Hī ðā hrēowigmōde
wurpon hyra wæpen ofdūne,   gewitan him wērigferhðe
on flēam sceacan.   Him mon feaht on lāst,
mægenēacen folc,   oð se mæsta dæl
þæs heriges læg   hilde gesæged
295 on ðām sigewonge,   sweordum gehēawen,
wulfum tō willan,   and ēac wælgīfrum
fuglum tō frōfre.   Flugon ðā ðe lyfdon
lāðra linde.   Him on lāste fōr
swēot Ebrēa   sigore geweorðod,
300 dōme gedȳrsod;   him feng Dryhten God
fægre on fultum,   Frēa ælmihtig.
Hī ðā fromlīce   fāgum swyrdum
hæleð higerōfe   herpað worhton
þurh lāðra gemong,   linde hēowon,
305 scildburh scæron;   scēotend wæron
gūðe gegremede,   guman Ebrisce,
þegnas on ðā tīd   þearle gelyste
gārgewinnes.   Þær on grēot gefēoll
se hȳhsta dæl   hēafodgerīmes
310 Assīria   ealdorduguðe,
lāðan cynnes: lȳthwōn becōm
cwicera tō cȳððe.   Cirdon cynerōfe,
wiggend on wiðertrod,   wælscel oninnan,
rēocende hræw;   rūm wæs tō nimanne
315 londbūendum   on ðām lāðestan,
hyra ealdfēondum   unlyfigendum
heolfrig hererēaf,   hyrsta scȳne,
bord and brād swyrd,   brūne helmas,

---

297. MS has *lind* followed by one or two illegible letters. The reading *linde* has been attacked on the grounds that the sense requires 'shield-bearers' or the like; but perhaps the sense of *linde* can be extended to imply spears or weapons generally.

When we, oppressed with troubles, now must die,
Perish together in the strife. Here lies
Our ruler, cut down by the sword, beheaded.'
Grieving in heart they cast their weapons down,
Demoralised they hastened off in flight.
The mighty army fought them as they fled
Until the greater number of that host
Lay slain upon the field of victory,
Cut down by swords, a pleasure for the wolves
And comfort to the carnage-greedy birds.
Survivors fled the weapons of their foes.
The Hebrew army chased them, flushed with triumph,
Honoured by noble deeds. Almighty God,
The Lord and Ruler, gave them splendid help.
The gallant heroes with their treasured swords
Then bravely carved a warlike passage through
The crowd of enemies, they cleft the shields,
Cut through the shield-wall. All the Hebrew men,
The warriors, were furious with war,
The thanes at that time thoroughly desired
The clash of spears. There fell down in the dust
The greatest part of all their total strength,
The officers of the Assyrians,
The hostile people; very few got home
Alive. The warlike warriors turned back
In full retreat among the reeking corpses
And heaps of slain. The people now had time
To take from their most hated enemies,
Their ancient foes now destitute of life,
The gory booty and fair ornaments,
The shields and broad swords and the gleaming helmets,

JUDITH

dȳre mādmas.   Hæfdon dōmlīce
320 on ðām folcstede   fȳnd oferwunnen
ēðelweardas,   ealdhettende
swyrdum āswefede: hīe on swaðe reston,
þā ðe him tō līfe   lāðost wǣron
cwicera cynna.   Þā sēo cnēoris eall,
325 mǣgða mǣrost,   ānes mōnðes fyrst,
wlanc wundenlocc   wǣgon and lǣddon
tō ðǣre beorhtan byrig   Bēthūliam
helmas and hupseax,   hāre byrnan,
gūðsceorp gumena   golde gefrætewod,
330 mǣrra mādma   þonne mon ǣnig
āsecgan mæge   searoþoncelra;
eal þæt ðā ðēodguman   þrymme geēodon,
cēne under cumblum   on compwīge
þurh Iūdithe   glēawe lāre,
335 mægð mōdigre.   Hī tō mēde hyre
of ðām sīðfate   sylfre brōhton
eorlas æscrōfe   Hōlofernes
sweord and swātigne helm,   swylce ēac sīde byrnan,
gerēnode rēadum golde,   and eal þæt se rinca baldor
340 swīðmōd sinces āhte   oððe sundoryrfes,
bēaga and beorhtra māðma,   hī þæt þǣre beorhtan idese
āgēafon gearoþoncolre.   Ealles ðæs Iūdith sægde
wuldor weroda Dryhtne,   þe hyre weorðmynde geaf,
mǣrðe on moldan rīce,   swylce ēac mēde on heofonum,
345 sigorlēan in swegles wuldre   þæs ðe hēo āhte sōðne
geleafan
tō ðām Ælmihtigan;   hūru æt þām ende ne twēode
þæs lēanes þe hēo lange gyrnde.   Þæs sȳ ðām lēofan
Dryhtne
wuldor tō wīdan aldre,   þe gescēop wind and lyfte,
roderas and rūme grundas,   swylce ēac rēðe strēamas
350 and swegles drēamas   þurh his sylfes miltse.

350. 'boundless and eternal' added in translation.
156

The precious treasures. On the battle-field
They worthily had overcome their foes,
The owners of the land destroyed by swords
Their former enemies, those who alive
Had been most hateful of all living people
To them lay in their tracks. Then all the tribe,
Greatest of nations, for a whole month's space,
Proud, curly-haired, carried and bore away
To the fair city of Bethulia
Helmets and hip-swords and grey coats of armour,
The corslets of the men, adorned with gold,
And treasures more illustrious by far
Than any man however wise could say.
The warriors won all that by their might,
Bold under banners on the battle-field,
Through Judith's wise advice, courageous maid.
The hardy heroes from that venture brought
As a reward for her the bloody helmet
And sword of Holofernes, and his broad
Corslet, adorned with good red gold, and all
The treasure that the lord of warriors,
Proud man, had owned, all his inheritance,
His rings and gleaming treasures did they give
The fair wise lady. Judith for all this
Ascribed the glory to the Lord of hosts
Who gave her fame and honour in the world,
Likewise rewarded her in heaven above,
Repaid her in the glory of the sky
Because she had true faith in the Almighty.
She did not doubt that she would at the end
Have the reward that she had long desired.
For this may there be glory evermore
To the dear Lord who made the wind and air,
The heavens and the spacious grounds beneath,
The pouring waters and the heavenly joys
Through His own boundless and eternal mercy.

The Dream of the Rood

That this is the finest, most imaginately conceived and most original of the OE religious poems few will dispute. Some commentators have felt the standard of poetry in the latter part of the poem to fall gravely below that of the Dream itself; but it would be strange and improper for the intensity of the reflective re-action to match that of the deep religious experience.

The poem appears to be early, probably before 750, as passages from it are carved on the Ruthwell Cross, which the experts generally believe to have been carved then or earlier, for discussion of which see the editions listed below and further references there given.

BIBLIOGRAPHY

ASPR II

Bruce Dickins and A. S. C. Ross, *The Dream of the Rood*, Methuen's Old English Library, London, 1934

Michael Swanton, *The Dream of Rood*, Manchester, 1970

Pope, 7 OE P

Sweet ASR (complete only in Sweet/Whitelock)

R. Woolf, 'Doctrinal Influences on the *Dream of the Rood*', *Medium Ævum*, XXVII, 1958

J. A. Burrows, 'An Approach to the *Dream of the Rood*', *Neophilologus*, XLIII, 1959

The Dream of the Rood

Hwæt, ic swefna cyst   secgan wylle,
hwæt mē gemǣtte   tō midre nihte,
syðþan reordberend   reste wunedon.
Þūhte mē þæt ic gesāwe   syllicre trēow
5 on lyft lǣdan   lēohte bewunden,
bēama beorhtost.   Eall þæt bēacen wæs
begoten mid golde;   gimmas stōdon
fægere æt foldan scēatum,   swylce þǣr fīfe wǣron
uppe on þām eaxlegespanne.   Behēoldon þǣr engeldryhta
      feala
10 fægere þurh forðgesceaft;   ne wæs ðǣr hūru fracodes
      gealga,
ac hine þǣr behēoldon   hālige gāstas,
men ofer moldan,   and eall þēos mǣre gesceaft.
Syllic wæs se sigebēam   and ic synnum fāh,
forwunded mid wommum.   Geseah ic wuldres trēow
15 wǣdum geweorðod   wynnum scīnan,
gegyred mid golde;   gimmas hæfdon
bewrigen weorðlīce   Wealdendes trēow.
Hwæðre ic þurh þæt gold   ongytan meahte
earmra ǣrgewin,   þæt hit ǣrest ongan
20 swǣtan on þā swīðran healfe.   Eall ic wæs mid sorgum
      gedrēfed;
forht ic wæs for þǣre fægran gesyhðe.   Geseah ic þæt fūse
      bēacen
wendan wǣdum and blēom;   hwīlum hit wæs mid wǣtan
      bestēmed,
beswyled mid swātes gange,   hwīlum mid since gegyrwed.

2. *me gemǣtte*, literally 'I dreamed'.

9. *engeldryhta feala* MS *engel dryhtnes ealle*. The MS reading does not make sense. Dickins and Ross omit *ealle* and emend to *engeldryhte*, but Pope's proposal (*Rhythm of Beowulf*, p. 111, footnote), which is here adopted, is palaeographically preferable.

12–13 The two sentences are combined in the translation.

The Dream of the Rood

Hear while I tell about the best of dreams
Which came to me the middle of one night
While humankind were sleeping in their beds.
It was as though I saw a wondrous tree
Towering in the sky suffused with light,
Brightest of beams; and all that beacon was
Covered with gold. The corners of the earth
Gleamed with fair jewels, just as there were five
Upon the cross-beam. Many bands of angels,
Fair throughout all eternity, looked on.
No felon's gallows that, but holy spirits,
Mankind, and all this marvellous creation,
Gazed on the glorious tree of victory.
And I with sins was stained, wounded with guilt.
I saw the tree of glory brightly shine
In gorgeous clothing, all bedecked with gold.
The Ruler's tree was worthily adorned
With gems; yet I could see beyond that gold
The ancient strife of wretched men, when first
Upon its right side it began to bleed.
I was all moved with sorrows, and afraid
At the fair sight. I saw that lively beacon
Changing its clothes and hues; sometimes it was
Bedewed with blood and drenched with flowing gore,
At other times it was bedecked with treasure.
So I lay watching there the Saviour's tree,

Hwæðre ic þær licgende   lange hwīle
25 behēold hrēowcearig   Hǣlendes trēow
oð ðæt ic gehȳrde   þæt hit hlēoðrode.
Ongan þā word sprecan   wudu sēlesta:
'Þæt wæs gēara iū,   ic þæt gȳta geman,
þæt ic wæs āhēawen   holtes on ende,
30 āstyred of stefne mīnum.   Genāman mē ðær strange
feondas,
geworhton him þær tō wǣfersȳne,   hēton mē heora
wergas hebban.
Bǣron mē þær beornas on eaxlum   oð ðæt hīe mē on
beorg āsetton,
gefæstnodon mē þær fēondas genōge.   Geseah ic þā
Frēan mancynnes
efstan elne micle   þæt Hē mē wolde on gestīgan.
35 Þær ic þā ne dorste   ofer Dryhtnes word
būgan oððe berstan   þā ic bifian geseah
eorðan scēatas.   Ealle ic mihte
fēondas gefyllan,   hwæðre ic fæste stōd.
Ongyrede Hine þā geong hæleð   þæt wæs God ælmihtig,
40 strang and stīðmōd;   gestāh Hē on gealgan hēanne,
mōdig on manigra gesyhðe,   þā Hē wolde mancyn lȳsan.
Bifode ic þā mē se beorn ymbclypte;   ne dorste ic
hwæðre būgan tō eorðan,
feallan tō foldan scēatum,   ac ic sceolde fæste standan.
Rōd wæs ic ārǣred;   āhōf ic rīcne Cyning,
45 heofona Hlāford,   hyldan mē ne dorste.
Þurhdrifan hī mē mid deorcan næglum,   on mē syndon
þā dolg gesīene,
opene inwidhlemmas.   Ne dorste ic hira ǣnigum sceððan.
Bysmeredon hīe unc būtu ætgædere.   Eall ic wæs mid
blōde bestēmed,
begoten of þæs guman sīdan   siððan Hē hæfde His
gāst onsended.
50 Feala ic on þām beorge   gebiden hæbbe
wrāðra wyrda.   Geseah ic weruda God

Grieving in spirit for a long, long while,
Until I heard it utter sounds, the best
Of woods began to speak these words to me:
'It was long past—I still remember it—
That I was cut down at the copse's end,
Moved from my roots. Strong enemies there took me,
Told me to hold aloft their criminals,
Made me a spectacle. Men carried me
Upon their shoulders, set me on a hill,
A host of enemies there fastened me.
And then I saw the Lord of all mankind
Hasten with eager zeal that He might mount
Upon me. I durst not against God's word
Bend down or break, when I saw tremble all
The surface of the earth. Although I might
Have struck down all the foes, yet stood I fast.
Then the young hero (who was God Almighty)
Got ready, resolute and strong in heart.
He climbed onto the lofty gallows-tree,
Bold in the sight of many watching men,
When He intended to redeem mankind.
I trembled as the warrior embraced me.
But still I dared not bend down to the earth,
Fall to the ground. Upright I had to stand.
A rood I was raised up; and I held high
The noble King, the Lord of heaven above.
I dared not stoop. They pierced me with dark nails;
The scars can still be clearly seen on me,
The open wounds of malice. Yet might I
Not harm them. They reviled us both together.
I was made wet all over with the blood
Which poured out from His side, after He had
Sent forth His spirit. And I underwent
Full many a dire experience on that hill.
I saw the God of hosts stretched grimly out.

þearle þenian;   þ̄ystro hæfdon
bewrigen mid wolcnum   Wealdendes hrǣw,
scīrne scīman   sceadu forðēode,
55 wann under wolcnum.   Wēop eal gesceaft,
cwīðdon Cyninges fyll.   Crīst wæs on rōde.
Hwæðere þǣr fūse   feorran cwōman
tō þām æðelinge;   ic þæt eall behēold.
Sāre ic wæs mid sorgum gedrēfed,   hnāg ic hwæðre þām
secgum tō handa,
60 ēaðmōd elne mycle.   Genāmon hīe þǣr ælmihtigne God,
āhōfon Hine of ðām hefian wīte,   forlēton mē þā
hilderincas
standan stēame bedrifenne;   eall ic wæs mid strǣlum
forwundod.
Ālēdon Hine ðǣr limwērigne,   gestōdon Him æt His
līces hēafdum,
behēoldon hīe ðǣr heofenes Dryhten,   and Hē Hine ðǣr
hwīle reste,
65 mēðe æfter ðām miclan gewinne.   Ongunnon Him þā
moldern wyrcan
beornas on banan gesyhðe,   curfon hīe ðǣt of beorhtan
stāne,
gesetton hīe ðǣron sigora Wealdend.   Ongunnon Him þā
sorhlēoð galan
earme on þā æfentīde.   Þā hīe woldon eft sīðian
mēðe fram þām mǣran Þēodne,   reste Hē ðǣr mǣte
weorode.

63. *hine ðær* MS *hie ðær*, Ruthwell Cross *hiæ hinæ*. The MS reading is acceptable, but some editors have felt that the accusative should be expressed rather than understood. Sweet therefore takes *hie hine* from the Ruthwell Cross. *hine ðær* equally overcomes the difficulty, as the scribe could have caught *hie* from the following line. The nominative does not need here to be expressed.

66. *banan*, singular, can only refer to the Cross. C. L. Wrenn (*Beowulf*, p. 306, s.v. *wyrsan*) argues that *banan* is a late WS genitive plural and explains similarly *guman*, l. 146.

69. *mæte weorode*, a rather weak litotes for 'alone', see l. 124.

Darkness covered the Ruler's corpse with clouds,
His shining beauty; shadows passed across,
Black in the darkness. All creation wept,
Bewailed the King's death; Christ was on the cross.
And yet I saw men coming from afar,
Hastening to the Prince. I watched it all.
With sorrows I was grievously oppressed,
Yet willingly I bent to those men's hands,
Humbly. They took up there Almighty God,
And from the heavy torment lifted Him.
The soldiers left me standing drenched with moisture,
Wounded all over with the metal points.
They laid Him down limb-weary; then they stood
Beside the corpse's head, there they beheld
The Lord of heaven, and He rested there
A while, tired after the great agony.
The men then made a sepulchre for Him
In sight of me. They carved it of bright stone,
And set therein the Lord of victories.
Next, wretched in the eventide, they sang
A dirge for Him; and when they went away,
Weary from that great Prince, He stayed, alone.

70 Hwæðere wē ðǣr grēotende gōde hwīle
stōdon on staðole, stefn up gewāt
hilderinca; hrǣw cōlode,
fæger feorgbold. Þā ūs man fyllan ongan
ealle tō eorðan; þæt wæs egeslic wyrd.
75 Bedealf ūs man on dēopan sēaþe; hwæðre mē þǣr
                                         Dryhtnes þegnas,
frēondas gefrūnon,
gvredon mē golde and seolfre.
    Nū ðū miht gehȳran, hæleð mīn se lēofa,
þæt ic bealuwara weorc gebiden hæbbe,
80 sārra sorga. Is nū sǣl cumen
þæt mē weorðiað wīde and sīde
menn ofer moldan and eall þēos mǣre gesceaft,
gebiddaþ him tō þyssum bēacne. On mē Bearn Godes
þrōwode hwīle; for þan ic þrymfæst nū
85 hlīfige under heofenum, and ic hǣlan mæg
ǣghwylcne ānra þāra þe him bið egesa tō mē.
Iū ic wæs geworden wīta heardost,
lēodum lāðost, ǣr þan ic him līfes weg
rihtne gerȳmde reordberendum.
90 Hwæt mē þā geweorðode wuldres Ealdor
ofer holtwudu, heofonrīces Weard,
swylce swā Hē his mōdor ēac, Mārian sylfe,
ælmihtig God for ealle men
geweorðode ofer eall wīfa cynn.
95   Nū ic þē hāte, hæleð mīn se lēofa,
þæt ðū þās gesyhðe secge mannum,
onwrēoh wordum þæt hit is wuldres bēam,
se ðe ælmihtig God on þrōwode
for mancynnes manegum synnum

---

71. MS *syððan up gewat* makes no sense. Some editors insert *stefn* after
syððan, which makes good sense but is metrically abnormal. *stefn* for *syððan*
remains the best suggestion.

Yet we remained there weeping in our places
A good long time after the warriors' voices
Had passed away from us. The corpse grew cold,
The fair abode of life. Then men began
To cut us down. That was a dreadful fate.
In a deep pit they buried us. But friends
And servants of the Lord learnt where I was,
And decorated me with gold and silver.
Now you may understand, dear warrior,
That I have suffered deeds of wicked men
And grievous sorrows. Now the time has come
That far and wide on earth men honour me,
And all this great and glorious creation,
And to this beacon offer prayers. On me
The Son of God once suffered; therefore now
I tower mighty underneath the heavens,
And I may heal all those in awe of me.
Once I became the cruellest of tortures,
Most hateful to all nations, till the time
I opened the right way of life for men.
So then the Prince of glory honoured me,
And heaven's King exalted me above
All other trees, just as Almighty God
Raised up His mother Mary for all men
Above all other women in the world.
Now, my dear warrior, I order you
That you reveal this vision to mankind,
Declare in words this is the tree of glory
On which Almighty God once suffered torments
For mankind's many sins, and for the deeds

100 and Ādōmes   ealdgewyrhtum.

Dēað Hē þær byrigde,   hwæðere eft Dryhten ārās
mid His miclan mihte   mannum tō helpe.

Hē ðā on heofenas āstāg;   hider eft fundaþ
on þysne middangeard   mancynn sēcan
105 on dōmdæge   Dryhten sylfa,
ælmihtig God   and His englas mid,
þæt Hē þonne wile dēman,   se āh dōmes geweald,
ānra gehwylcum   swā hē him ǣrur hēr
on þyssum lǣnum   līfe geearnaþ.
110 Ne mæg þær ænig   unforht wesan
for þām worde   þe se Wealdend cwyð.

Frīneð Hē for þǣre mænige   hwǣr se man sīe,
se ðe for Dryhtnes naman   dēaðes wolde
biteres onbyrigan   swā Hē ǣr on ðām bēame dyde.
115 Ac hīe þonne forhtiað   and fēa þencaþ
hwæt hīe tō Crīste   cweðan onginnen.

Ne þearf ðǣr þonne ænig   anforht wesan
þe him ǣr in brēostum bereð   bēacna sēlest,
ac ðurh ðā rōde sceal   rīce gesēcan
120 of eorðwege   æghwylc sāwl,
sēo þe mid Wealdende   wunian þenceð.'

Gebæd ic mē þā tō þān bēame   blīðe mōde,
elne mycle,   þær ic āna wæs
mǣte werede;   wæs mōdsefa
125 āfȳsed on forðwege,   feala ealra gebād
langunghwīla.   Is mē nū līfes hyht
þæt ic þone sigebēam   sēcan mōte
āna oftor   þonne ealle men,
well weorþian.   Mē is willa tō ðām
130 mycel on mōde,   and mīn mundbyrd is
geriht tō þǣre rōde.   Nāh ic rīcra feala
frēonda on foldan,   ac hīe forð heonon
gewiton of worulde drēamum,   sōhton him wuldres
Cyning,
lifiaþ nū on heofenum   mid Hēahfædere,

Of Adam long ago. He tasted death
Thereon; and yet the Lord arose again
By His great might to come to human aid.
He rose to heaven. And the Lord Himself,
Almighty God and all His angels with Him,
Will come onto this earth again to seek
Mankind on Doomsday, when the final Judge
Will give His verdict upon every man,
What in this fleeting life he shall have earned.
Nor then may any man be without fear
About the words the Lord shall say to him.
Before all He shall ask where that man is
Who for God's name would suffer bitter death
As formerly He did upon the cross.
Then will they be afraid, and few will know
What they may say to Christ. But there need none
Be fearful if he bears upon his breast
The best of tokens. Through the cross each soul
May journey to the heavens from this earth,
Who with the Ruler thinks to go and dwell.'
I prayed then to the cross with joyous heart
And eagerness, where I was all alone,
Companionless; my spirit was inspired
With keenness for departure; and I spent
Much time in longing. Now my hope in life
Is that I may approach the tree of triumph
Alone more often than all other men,
Honour it well; my wish for that is great
Within my heart, and my hope for support
Is turned towards the cross. I have on earth
Not many noble friends, but they have gone
Hence from earth's joys and sought the King of glory.
With the High Father now they live in heaven

135 wuniaþ on wuldre;   and ic wēne mē
daga gehwylce   hwænne mē Dryhtnes rōd,
þe ic hēr on eorðan   ǣr scēawode,
on þysson lǣnan   līfe gefetige
and mē þonne gebringe   þǣr is blis mycel,
140 drēam on heofonum,   þǣr is Dryhtnes folc
geseted tō symle,   þǣr is singāl blis,
and mē þonne āsette   þǣr ic syþþan mōt
wunian on wuldre   well mid þām hālgum,
drēames brūcan.   Sī mē Dryhten frēond,
145 se ðe hēr on eorðan   ǣr þrōwode
on þām gealgtrēowe   for guman synnum.
Hē ūs onlȳsde   and ūs līf forgeaf,
heofonlicne hām.   Hiht wæs genīwad
mid blēdum and mid blisse   þām þe þǣr bryne þolodan.
150 Se Sunu wæs sigorfæst   on þām sīðfate,
mihtig and spēdig,   þā Hē mid manigeo cōm,
gāsta weorode,   on Godes rīce,
Anwealda ælmihtig,   englum tō blisse
and eallum ðām hālgum   þām þe on heofonum ǣr
155 wunedon on wuldre,   þā heora Wealdend cwōm,
ælmihtig God,   þǣr His ēðel wæs.

146. *guman*. Cook and Sweet emend to *gumena*, but a collective sense is
possible. See note to l. 66 above for a suggestion by Wrenn.
148–51. This passage refers to the Harrowing of Hell.

And dwell in glory; and I wait each day
For when the cross of God, which here on earth
I formerly beheld, may fetch me from
This transitory life and carry me
To where there is great bliss and joy in heaven,
Where the Lord's host is seated at the feast,
And it shall set me where I afterwards
May dwell in glory, live in lasting bliss
Among the saints. May God be friend to me,
He who once suffered on the gallows tree
On earth here for men's sins. Us He redeemed
And granted us our life and heavenly home.
Hope was renewed with glory and with bliss
For those who suffered burning fires in hell.
The Son was mighty on that expedition,
Successful and victorious; and when
The one Almighty Ruler brought with Him
A multitude of spirits to God's kingdom,
To bliss among the angels and the souls
Of all who dwelt already in the heavens
In glory, then Almighty God had come,
The Ruler entered into His own land.

The Wanderer

It is now generally agreed that *The Wanderer* is a complete poem dealing in a consistently Christian manner with a coherent theme. Agreement in detail about the theme and structure is however lacking, and the literature on the poem is copious and shows no sign of abating. A summary of my interpretation follows. The paradox is propounded that despite the hardships of his life the lonely exile often feels the grace of God (ll. 1–5). Someone then narrates his personal experiences of exile (ll. 8–29), which he gives a more general application by appealing to others who have had similar experiences (ll. 29–57). This consideration leads him to feel that he cannot understand why in the face of so much suffering and the general prospect of decay he is not depressed (ll. 58–63). Various precepts are advanced about how one should live, leading to the statement that one must understand the nature of the end of the world, of which the present signs of decline and the historical example of the Flood are tokens (ll. 64–87).* He who has thought deeply about all this may well ask: 'Where have all the former glories of earth gone? Only ruins and the dark and cold remain. Everything earthly is transitory' (ll. 88–110). It will be well for those with faith, for all our security is with God (ll. 111–115).

Even if one disagrees in detail with the line of thought sketched in this summary, some such coherent theme can be seen to work through the poem. The problems are greatly increased by the uncertainty about where the speeches in the poem begin and end. The punctuation of the manuscript gives no help, and it is worth remembering that the placing of inverted commas in the editions is purely according to the opinion of the editors. There are three

* J. A. Burrow, '*The Wanderer:* ll. 73-87', *Notes and Queries*, N.S. xii, 1965.

clues, at ll. 6, 91, and 111. The second of these is unambiguous: a speech is about to begin. The other two could mean that a speech has ended or is about to begin, or even that it has already begun and is going to continue. The word *cwæð* at l. 111 may mean that the speech which began at l. 92 has ended, but it is strange that l. 91 has *ācwið* in the present whereas *cwæð* is past. Most of the suggestions which have been advanced are listed here: a speech begins at l. 8, or at l. 1 and continues at l. 8; this speech ends during l. 29 or at l. 57 or l. 63 or l. 87 or l. 110 or l. 115, in the last two cases containing another speech; the speech beginning at l. 92 ends at l. 110 or l. 96; or the whole poem may be one speech containing another with the exception of stage directions at ll. 6–7 and 111; or the whole poem may be a dramatic monologue containing two reported speeches ll. 1–5 and ll. 92–110. I offer the last suggestion and have printed it so, but the reader must make his own decision.

It is surprising that the first separate edition of this poem was that of R. F. Leslie in 1966. The second, by T. P. Dunning and A. J. Bliss, has appeared since this book first went to the printers. These two editions are invaluable to anyone who takes a serious interest in the poem. Between them they supply a full and up to date bibliography and summarise all the earlier disputes, adding important new suggestions.

BIBLIOGRAPHY

Kershaw
ASPR III
Sweet ASR
R. F. Leslie, *The Wanderer*, Manchester, 1966
T. P. Dunning and A. J. Bliss, *The Wanderer*, Methuen's Old English Library, London, 1969

'Oft him anhaga   āre gebīdeð,
Metudes miltse,   þēah þe hē mōdcearig
geond lagulāde   longe sceolde
hrēran mid hondum   hrīmcealde sǣ,
5 wadan wræclāstas;   wyrd bið ful ārǣd.'
Swā cwæð eardstapa   earfeða gemyndig,
wrāþra wælsleahta,   winemǣga hryre.
    Oft ic sceolde āna   ūhtna gehwylce
mīne ceare cwīþan.   Nis nū cwicra nān
10 þe ic him mōdsefan   mīnne durre
sweotule āsecgan.   Ic tō sōþe wāt
þæt bið in eorle   indryhten þēaw
þæt hē his ferðlocan   fæste binde,
healde his hordcofan,   hycge swā hē wille.
15 Ne mæg wērigmōd   wyrde wiðstondan,
ne se hrēo hyge   helpe gefremman.
For ðon dōmgeorne   drēorigne oft
in hyra brēostcofan   bindað fæste.
Swā ic mōdsefan   mīnne sceolde,
20 oft earmcearig,   ēðle bidǣled,
frēomǣgum feor,   feterum sǣlan,
siþþan gēara iū   goldwine mīnne
hrūsan heolstre biwrāh   and ic hēan þonan
wōd wintercearig   ofer waþema gebind,

---

1. *gebideð.* Editors and translators have variously stated or implied that this form is part of *gebidan* or *gebiddan*, and there is further disagreement about whether the ge- makes the verb perfective. The *þeah þe* clause makes it clear that the sentence is a paradox, so we can dismiss those interpretations which give 'waits for, prays for, seeks for' etc., as no Christian would be surprised that one should wait, pray or seek for God's grace when surrounded by hardship; but it would be important and interesting that one should *experience* grace despite earthly troubles.

6. Whether *swa cwæð* means a speech precedes or follows has been much but inconclusively debated.

The Wanderer

'Often the solitary man enjoys
The grace and mercy of the Lord, though he
Careworn has long been forced to stir by hand
The ice-cold sea on many waterways,
Travel the exile's path; fate is relentless.'
So spoke a wanderer who called to mind
Hardships and cruel wars and deaths of lords.
Frequently have I had to mourn alone
My cares each morning; now no living man
Exists to whom I dare reveal my heart
Openly; and I know it for a truth
That in a man it is a noble virtue
To hide his thoughts, lock up his private feelings,
However he may feel. A weary heart
Cannot oppose inexorable fate,
And anxious thoughts can bring no remedy.
And so those jealous of their reputation
Often bind fast their sadness in their breasts.
So I, careworn, deprived of fatherland,
Far from my noble kin, have often had
To tie in fetters my own troubled spirit,
Since long ago I wrapped my lord's remains
In darkness of the earth, and sadly thence
Journeyed by winter over icy waves,

25 sōhte sele drēorig   sinces bryttan,
    hwǣr ic feor oþþe nēah   findan meahte
    þone þe in meoduhealle   mīn mine wisse,
    oþþe mec frēondlēasne   frēfran wolde,
    wēman mid wynnum.   Wāt se þe cunnað
30 hū slīþen bið   sorg tō gefēran
    þām þe him lȳt hafað   lēofra geholena;
    warað hine wræclāst,   nāles wunden gold,
    ferðloca frēorig,   nālæs foldan blǣd;
    gemon hē selesecgas   and sincþege,
35 hū hine on geoguðe   his goldwine
    wenede tō wiste;   wyn eal gedrēas.
    For þon wāt se þe sceal   his winedryhtnes
    lēofes lārcwidum   longe forþōlian,
    ðonne sorg and slǣp   somod ætgædre
40 earmne ānhogan   oft gebindað:
    þinceð him on mōde   þæt hē his mondryhten
    clyppe and cysse   and on cnēo lecge
    honda and hēafod,   swā hē hwīlum ǣr
    in gēardagum   giefstōles brēac;
45 ðonne onwæcneð eft   winelēas guma,
    gesihð him biforan   fealwe wēgas,
    baþian brimfuglas,   brǣdan feþra,
    hrēosan hrīm and snāw   hagle gemenged.
    Þonne bēoð þȳ hefigran   heortan benne,
50 sāre æfter swǣsne.   Sorg bið genīwad
    þonne māga gemynd   mōd geondhweorfeð,
    grēteð glīwstafum,   georne geondscēawað.
    Secga geseldan   swimmað oft on weg,
    flēotendra ferð   nō þǣr fela bringeð
55 cūðra cwidegiedda.   Cearo bið genīwad
    þām þe sendan sceal   swīþe geneahhe
    ófer waþema gebind   wērigne sefan.

Paths of exile [margin annotation beside lines 32–33]

41–4. Translation paraphrased to clarify the nature of the ritual described.

And suffering sought the hall of a new patron,
If I in any land might find one willing
To show me recognition in his mead-hall,
Comfort my loneliness, tempt me with pleasures.
He knows who has experienced it how bitter
Is sorrow as a comrade to the man
Who lacks dear human friends; fair twisted gold
Is not for him, but rather paths of exile,
Coldness of heart for the gay countryside.
He calls to mind receiving gifts of treasure
And former hall-retainers, and remembers
How in his younger years his lordly patron
Was wont to entertain him at the feast.
Now all that joy has gone. He understands
Who long must do without the kind advice
Of his beloved lord, while sleep and sorrow
Together often bind him, sad and lonely,
How in his mind it seems that he embraces
And kisses his liege lord, and on his knee
Lays hand and head, as when he formerly
Received as a retainer in the hall
Gifts from the throne; but then the joyless man
Wakes up and sees instead the yellow waves,
The sea-birds bathing, stretching out their wings,
While snow and hail and frost fall all together.
The heart's wounds seem by that yet heavier,
Grief for the dear one gone: care is renewed,
When memories of kinsmen fill the mind,
He greets them gladly, contemplates them keenly,
But his old friends swim frequently away;
The floating spirits bring him all too few
Of the old well-known songs; care is renewed
For him who must continually send
His weary spirit over icy waves.

For þon ic geþencan ne mæg   geond þās woruld
for hwan mōdsefa   mīn ne gesweorce
60 þonne ic eorla līf   eal geondþence,
hū hī fǣrlīce   flet ofgēafon,
mōdge maguþegnas.   Swā þes middangeard
ealra dōgra gehwām   drēoseð and fealleþ.
For þon ne mæg weorþan wīs   wer ǣr hē āge
65 wintra dǣl in woruldrīce.   Wita sceal geþyldig,
ne sceal nō tō hātheort   ne tō hrædwyrde,
ne tō wāc wiga   ne tō wanhȳdig,
ne tō forht ne tō fægen   ne tō feohgīfre,
ne nǣfre gielpes tō georn   ǣr hē geare cunne.
70 Beorn sceal gebīdan   þonne hē bēot spriceð
oþ þæt collenferð   cunne gearwe
hwider hreþra gehygd   hweorfan wille.
Ongietan sceal glēaw hæle   hū gæstlic bið
þonne eall þisse worulde wela   wēste stondeð,
75 swā nū missenlīce   geond þisne middangeard
winde biwāune   weallas stondaþ,
hrīme bihrorene,   hryðge þā ederas.
Wōriað þā wīnsalo,   waldend licgað
drēame bidrorene,   duguð eal gecrong,
80 wlonc bī wealle.   Sume wīg fornōm,
ferede in forðwege;   sumne fugel oþbær
ofer hēanne holm;   sumne se hāra wulf
dēaðe gedǣlde;   sumne drēorighlēor
in eorðscræfe   eorl gehȳdde.

71–2. I have expanded the translation to clarify what I believe these
lines to mean.

Therefore I see no reason in the world
Why my heart grows not dark, when I consider
The lives of warriors, how they suddenly
Have left their hall, the bold and noble thanes,
Just as this earth and everything thereon
Declines and weakens each and every day.
Certainly no man may be wise before
He's lived his share of winters in the world.
A wise man must be patient, not too hasty
In speech, or passionate, impetuous
Or timid as a fighter, nor too anxious
Or carefree or too covetous of wealth;
Nor ever must he be too quick to boast
Before he's gained experience of himself.
A man should wait, before he makes a vow,
Until in pride he truly can assess
How, when a crisis comes, he will re-act.
The wise must know how awesome it will be
When all the wealth of earth stands desolate,
As now in various parts throughout the world
Stand wind-blown walls, frost-covered, ruined buildings.
The wine-halls crumble; monarchs lifeless lie,
Deprived of pleasures, all the doughty troop   *mutability*
Dead by the wall; some battle carried off.
Took from this world; one the dire bird removed
Over the ocean deep; one the grey wolf
Consigned to death; and one a tear-stained hero

85 Ȳþde swā þisne eardgeard   ælda Scyppend
oþ þæt burgwara   breahtma lēase
eald enta geweorc   īdlu stōdon.

Se þonne þisne wealsteal   wīse geþōhte
and þis deorce līf   dēope geondþenceð,
90 frōd in ferðe   feor oft gemon
wælsleahta worn,   and þās word ācwið:
'Hwǣr cwōm mearg, hwǣr cwōm mago?   Hwǣr cwōm
māþþumgyfa?
Hwǣr cwōm symbla gesetu?   Hwǣr sindon seledrēamas?
Ēalā beorht būne,   ēalā byrnwiga,
95 ēalā þēodnes þrym.   Hū sēo þrāg gewāt,
genāp under nihthelm   swā hēo nō wǣre.
Stondeð nū on lāste   lēofre duguþe
weal wundrum hēah   wyrmlīcum fāh.
Eorlas fornōmon   asca þrȳþe,
100 wǣpen wælgīfru,   wyrd sēo mǣre,
and þās stānhleoþu   stormas cnyssað.
Hrīð hrēosende   hrūsan bindeð,
wintres wōma,   þonne won cymeð,
nīpeð nihtscūa,   norþan onsendeð
105 hrēo hæglfare   hæleþum on andan.
Eall is earfoðlic   eorþan rīce;
onwendeð wyrda gesceaft   weoruld under heofonum.
Hēr bið feoh lǣne,   hēr bið frēond lǣne,
hēr bið mon lǣne,   hēr bið mǣg lǣne.
110 Eal þis eorþan gesteal   īdel weorþeð.'
Swā cwǣð snottor on mōde,   gesæt him sundor æt rūne.

87. *eald enta geweorc.* Large ancient buildings and ruins were often
described as 'the works of giants', e.g. *Ruin*, l. 2, *Gnomic Verses*, l. 2. In
this case the giants may be literally intended. J. A. Burrow reasons that
since *stodon* is a preterite the sense of ll. 85–7 must all be in the past, and
the only destruction of this *eardgeard* that could be meant is the Flood. The
giants of *Genesis* vi. 4 were known to the Anglo-Saxons, and it was their
geweorc that stood idle.

111. *æt rune* omitted in translation. Its meaning is not clear; perhaps
'in meditation'.

Concealed from daylight in an earthy cave.
Just so in days long past mankind's Creator
Destroyed this earth, till lacking the gay sounds
Of citizens the ancient works of giants
Stood desolate. He who has wisely thought
And carefully considered this creation
And this dark life, experienced in spirit
Has often pondered many massacres
In far off ages, and might say these words:
'Where is the horse now, where the hero gone?
Where is the bounteous lord, and where the benches
For feasting? Where are all the joys of hall?
Alas for the bright cup, the armoured warrior,
The glory of the prince. That time is over,
Passed into night as it had never been.
Stands now memorial to that dear band
The splendid lofty wall, adorned with shapes
Of serpents; but the strong blood-greedy spear
And mighty destiny removed the heroes,
And storms now strike against these stony slopes.
The falling tempest binds in winter's vice
The earth, and darkness comes with shades of night,
And from the north fierce hail is felt to fall
In malice against men. And all is hardship
On earth, the immutable decree of fate
Alters the world which lies beneath the heavens.
Here property and friendship pass away,
Here man himself and kinsmen pass away,
And all this earthly structure comes to nought.'
Thus spoke the thoughtful sage, he sat apart.

Til biþ se þe his trēowe gehealdeþ;   ne sceal nǣfre his
                  torn tō rycene
beorn of his brēostum ācȳþan,   nemþe hē ǣr þā bōte
                   cunne,
eorl mid elne gefremman.   Wel bið þām þe him āre sēceð,
115 frōfre tō Fæder on heofonum,   þǣr ūs eal sēo fæstnung
                   stondeð.

Blessed is he who keeps his faith; a man
Must never be too eager to reveal
His cares, unless he knows already how
To bring about a cure by his own zeal.
Well shall it be for him who looks for grace
And comfort from our father in the heavens,
Where is ordained all our security.

The Seafarer

The Seafarer has a literature about as extensive as that of *The Wanderer*, with which it has certain similarities, on which however it would be dangerous to build too much. The main problems are, first that the poem appears to fall into two unconnected halves with a break in the middle of l. 64, all before being about seafaring while the rest is clearly homiletic, and second that within the first part there appear to be expressed two incompatible attitudes to the sea. The generally accepted answer to the first problem is that the first part of the poem gives a situation on which the homiletic section is based. This makes very good sense, and the correspondence between the discussion of abodes in the first part, ll. 5, 13, 30, 38, and 57 with the reference to our heavenly home at ll. 117 ff. gives strong support. In her edition Mrs. I. L. Gordon does much to abolish the break in l. 64 by placing there a comma with the sentence ending in the middle of l. 66. The problem of the divergent attitudes in the first part caused early commentators to postulate a dialogue between an old and a young sailor, and Professor J. C. Pope has come to a similar conclusion in a recent study. It is however now generally agreed that the poem is a monologue, and that the paradox is one that could well exist in one man's mind, a love of the sea despite an understanding of its hardships and dangers. If this be accepted the only remaining difficulty is the word *sylf* at l. 35, which appears contextually not to fit in with such an interpretation. It has led to such suggestions as that the speaker had hitherto only been on coastal trips and now planned to make a more ambitious journey across the sea. The first part has variously been regarded as literal or allegorical, and related to such figures as the pilgrim.

BIBLIOGRAPHY

Kershaw

ASPR III

Sweet ASR

I. L. Gordon, *The Seafarer*, Methuen's Old English Library, London, 1960

S. B. Greenfield, 'The Old English Elegies', in E. G. Stanley, *Continuations and Beginnings*, London, 1966. The bibliography of this study lists the important work since Mrs. Gordon's edition.

The Seafarer

Mæg ic be mē sylfum   sōðgied wrecan,
sīþas secgan,   hū ic geswincdagum
earfoðhwīle   oft þrōwade,
bitre brēostceare   gebiden hæbbe,
5 gecunnad in cēole   cearselda fela,
atol ȳþa gewealc,   þǣr mec oft bigeat
nearo nihtwaco   æt nacan stefnan
þonne hē be clifum cnossað.   Calde geþrungen
wǣron mīne fēt,   forste gebunden
10 caldum clommum.   Þǣr þā ceare seofedun
hāt ymb heortan,   hungor innan slāt
merewērges mōd.   Þæt se mon ne wāt
þe him on foldan   fægrost limpeð
hū ic earmcearig   īscealdne sǣ
15 winter wunade   wræccan lāstum
winemǣgum bidroren,   *pause*
bihongen hrīmgicelum.   Hægl scūrum flēag.
Þǣr ic ne gehȳrde   būtan hlimman sǣ,
īscaldne wǣg.   Hwīlum ylfete song
20 dyde ic mē tō gomene,   ganetes hlēoþor
and huilpan swēg   fore hleahtor wera,
mǣw singende   fore medodrince.
Stormas þǣr stānclifu bēotan   þǣr him stearn oncwæð
īsigfeþera;   ful oft þæt earn bigeal
25 hyrnednebba.   Nǣnig hlēomǣga
fēasceaftig ferð   frēfran meahte.
For þon him gelȳfeð lȳt,   se þe āh līfes wyn
gebiden in burgum,   bealosīþa hwōn,

10. *seofedun*, literally 'lamented'.
21. 'missing' added in translation.
25. *hyrnednebba*, MS *urigfeþra*. The MS reading does not alliterate and is improbable after l. 24 *isigfeþera*. M. E. Goldsmith, 'The Seafarer and the Birds', *Review of English Studies*, N.S., V, 1954, proposed *hyrnednebba*, suggested by *Judith* l. 212 etc.

The Seafarer

I sing my own true story, tell my travels, *repetition*
How I have often suffered times of hardship
In days of toil, and have experienced
Bitter anxiety, my troubled home
On many a ship has been the heaving waves,
Where grim night-watch has often been my lot
At the ship's prow as it beat past the cliffs.
Oppressed by cold my feet were bound by frost
In icy bonds, while worries simmered hot
About my heart, and hunger from within
Tore the sea-weary spirit. He knows not,
Who lives most easily on land, how I
Have spent my winter on the ice-cold sea,
Wretched and anxious, in the paths of exile,
Lacking dear friends, hung round by icicles,
While hail flew past in showers. There heard I nothing
But the resounding sea, the ice-cold waves.
Sometimes I made the song of the wild swan
My pleasure, or the gannet's call, the cries
Of curlews for the missing mirth of men,
The singing gull instead of mead in hall.
Storms beat the rocky cliffs, and icy-winged
The tern replied, the horn-beaked eagle shrieked.
No patron had I there who might have soothed
My desolate spirit. He can little know
Who, proud and flushed with wine, has spent his time
With all the joys of life among the cities,

Cities founded by the King of men.

187

wlonc and wīngāl,   hū ic wērig oft
30 in brimlāde   bīdan sceolde.
Nāp nihtscūa,   norþan snīwde,
hrīm hrūsan bond,   hægl fēol on eorþan,
corna caldast.   For þon cnyssað nū
heortan geþōhtas   þæt ic hēan strēamas,
35 sealtȳþa gelāc,   sylf cunnige;
monað mōdes lust   mǣla gehwylce
ferð tō fēran   þæt ic feor heonan
elþēodigra   eard gesēce.
For þon nis þæs mōdwlonc   mon ofer eorþan,
40 ne his gifena þæs gōd,   ne in geoguþe tō þæs hwæt,
ne in his dǣdum tō þæs dēor,   ne him his dryhten tō
                            þæs hold,
þæt hē ā his sǣfōre   sorge næbbe
tō hwon hine Dryhten   gedōn wille.
Ne biþ him tō hearpan hyge,   ne tō hringþege,
45 ne tō wīfe wyn,   ne tō worulde hyht,
ne ymbe ōwiht elles   nefne ymb ȳða gewealc;
ac ā hafað longunge   se þe on lagu fundað.
Bearwas blōstmum nimað,   byrig fægriað,
wongas wlitigiað,   woruld ōnetteð;
50 ealle þā gemoniað   mōdes fūsne
sefan tō sīþe   þām þe swā þenceð
on flōdwegas   feor gewītan.
Swylce gēac monað   gēomran reorde,
singeð sumeres weard,   sorge bēodeð
55 bittre in brēosthord.   Þæt se beorn ne wāt,
sēftēadig secg,   hwæt þā sume drēogað
þe þā wræclāstas   wīdost lecgað.
For þon nū mīn hyge hweorfeð   ofer hreþerlocan,
mīn mōdsefa   mid mereflōde

---

35. *sylf* is difficult and gives support to those who wish to regard this part of the poem as a dialogue.

44. 'harmonious' added in translation.

Safe from such fearful venturings, how I
Have often suffered weary on the seas.
Night shadows darkened, snow came from the north,
Frost bound the earth and hail fell on the ground,
Coldest of corns. And yet the heart's desires
Incite me now that I myself should go
On towering seas, among the salt waves' play;
And constantly the heartfelt wishes urge
The spirit to venture, that I should go forth
To see the lands of strangers far away.
Yet no man in the world's so proud of heart,
So generous of gifts, so bold in youth,
In deeds so brave, or with so loyal lord,
That he can ever venture on the sea
Without great fears of what the Lord may bring.
His mind dwells not on the harmonious harp,
On ring-receiving, or the joy of woman,
Or wordly hopes, or anything at all
But the relentless rolling of the waves;
But he who goes to sea must ever yearn.
The groves bear blossom, cities grow more bright,
The fields adorn themselves, the world speeds up;
Yet all this urges forth the eager spirit
Of him who then desires to travel far
On the sea-paths. Likewise the cuckoo calls
With boding voice, the harbinger of summer
Offers but bitter sorrow in the breast.
The man who's blest with comfort does not know
What some then suffer who most widely travel
The paths of exile. Even now my heart
Journeys beyond its confines, and my thoughts

60 ofer hwæles ēþel   hweorfeð wīde
   eorþan scēatas,   cymeð eft tō mē
   gīfre and grǣdig;   gielleð ānfloga,
   hweteð on hwælweg   hreþer unwearnum
   ofer holma gelagu,   for þon mē hātran sind
65 Dryhtnes drēamas   þonne þis dēade līf
   lǣne on londe.   Ic gelȳfe nō
   þæt him eorðwelan   ēce stondað.
   Simle þrēora sum   þinga gehwylce
   ǣr his tīd āge   tō twēon weorþeð;
70 ādl oþþe yldo   oþþe ecghete
   fǣgum fromweardum   feorh oðþringeð.
   For þon biþ eorla gehwām   æftercweþendra
   lof lifgendra   lāstworda betst,
   þæt hē gewyrce,   ǣr hē onweg scyle,
75 fremum on foldan   wið fēonda nīþ
   dēorum dǣdum   dēofle tōgēanes,
   þæt hine ælda bearn   æfter hergen
   and his lof siþþan   lifge mid englum
   āwa tō ealdre,   ēcan līfes blǣd,

63. 'eager' added in translation.
hwælweg, MS *wælweg*. G. V. Smithers, 'The Meaning of *The Seafarer* and *The Wanderer*', *Medium Ævum*, XXVI, 1957, has ably defended the MS reading, but the rejection of his arguments in Gordon's notes carries more conviction.

64. Most editors put a full stop in mid-line, but Gordon's comma, earlier proposed by S. O. Andrew, *Style and Syntax in Old English*, New York, 1940, p. 33, links the awareness of the joys of the Lord with the problem which occupies the earlier part of the poem and gives the whole a satisfactory thematic logic.

69. *tid age*, MS *tide ge*. The usual emendations are *tīd āgā*, which makes the half-line mean 'before his life departs', and *tīddege* or *tīddæge* meaning 'span of life'. This proposal gives 'before he may have his allotted span'.

Over the sea, across the whale's domain,
Travel afar the regions of the earth,
And then come back to me with greed and longing.
The cuckoo cries, incites the eager breast
On to the whale's roads irresistibly,
Over the wide expanses of the sea,
Because the joys of God mean more to me
Than this dead transitory life on land.
That earthly wealth lasts to eternity
I don't believe. Always one of three things
Keeps all in doubt until one's destined hour.
Sickness, old age, the sword, each one of these
May end the lives of doomed and transient men.
Therefore for every warrior the best
Memorial is the praise of living men
After his death, that ere he must depart
He shall have done good deeds on earth against
The malice of his foes, and noble works
Against the devil, that the sons of men
May after praise him, and his glory live
For ever with the angels in the splendour
Of lasting life, in bliss among those hosts.

80 drēam mid dugeþum.   Dagas sind gewitene,
  ealle onmēdlan   eorþan rīces.
  Nearon nū cyningas   ne cāseras
  ne goldgiefan   swylce iū wæron,
  þonne hī mæst mid him   mærþa gefremedon
85 and on dryhtlicestum   dōme lifdon.
  Gedroren is þēos duguð eal,   drēamas sind gewitene,
  wuniað þā wācran   and þās woruld healdaþ,
  brūcað þurh bisgo.   Blæd is gehnæged,
  eorþan indryhto   ealdað and sēarað,
90 swā nū monna gehwylc   geond middangeard;
  yldo him on fareð,   onsȳn blācað,
  gomelfeax gnornað,   wāt his iūwine,
  æþelinga bearn   eorþan forgiefene.
  Ne mæg him þonne se flæschoma   þonne him þæt feorg
                                        losað
95 ne swēte forswelgan   ne sār gefēlan
  ne hond onhrēran   ne mid hyge þencan.
  Þēah þe græf wille   golde strēgan
  brōþor his geborenum,   byrgan be dēadum
  māþmum mislicum   þæt hine mid wille,
100 ne mæg þære sāwle   þe biþ synna ful
  gold tō gēoce   for Godes egsan,
  þonne hē hit ær hȳdeð   þenden hē hēr leofað.
  Micel biþ se Meotudes egsa,   for þon hī sēo molde
                                        oncyrreð;
  se gestaþelade   stīþe grundas,
105 eorþan scēatas   and uprodor.
  Dol biþ se þe him his Dryhten ne ondrædeþ;   cymeð him
                                        se dēað unþinged.

80–90. Medieval man believed that he was living in the sixth of the
Seven Ages and that the earth had deteriorated and was deteriorating. See
the account of the Seven Ages by V. A. Kolve, *The Play Called Corpus
Christi*, London, 1966, Chapters III–V.

102. 'Ready before his death' added in translation.

The great old days have gone, and all the grandeur
Of earth; there are not Caesars now or kings
Or patrons such as once there used to be,
Amongst whom were performed most glorious deeds,
Who lived in lordliest renown. Gone now
Is all that host, the splendours have departed.
Weaker men live and occupy the world,
Enjoy it but with care. Fame is brought low,
Earthly nobility grows old, decays,
As now throughout this world does every man.
Age comes on him, his countenance grows pale,
Grey-haired he mourns, and knows his former lords,
The sons of princes, given to the earth.
Nor when his life slips from him may his body
Taste sweetness or feel pain or stir his hand
Or use his mind to think. And though a brother
May strew with gold his brother's grave, and bury
His corpse among the dead with heaps of treasure,
Wishing them to go with him, yet can gold
Bring no help to the soul that's full of sins,
Against God's wrath, although he hide it here
Ready before his death while yet he lives.
Great is the might of God, by which earth moves;
For He established its foundations firm,
The land's expanses, and the sky above.
Foolish is he who does not fear his Lord,
For death will come upon him unprepared.

Ēadig bið se þe ēaþmōd leofaþ;   cymeð him sēo ār of
                          heofonum;
Meotod him þæt mōd gestaþelað   for þon hē in His
                        meahte gelȳfeð.
Stīeran mon sceal strongum mōde,   and þæt on
                        staþelum healdan,
110 and gewis wērum,   wīsum clǣne.
Scyle monna gehwylc   mid gemete healdan
wiþ lēofne and wið lāþne   . . . . . . bealo,
þēah þe hē hine wille fȳres   fulne . . . . ,
oþþe on bǣle   forbærnedne
115 his geworhtne wine,   wyrd biþ swīþre,
Meotud meahtigra   þonne ǣnges monnes gehygd.
Uton wē hycgan   hwǣr wē hām āgen
and þonne geþencan   hū wē þider cumen,
and wē þonne ēac tilien   þæt wē tō mōten
120 in þā ēcan   ēadignesse,
þǣr is līf gelong   in lufan Dryhtnes,
hyht in heofonum.   Þæs sȳ þām Hālgan þonc
þæt Hē ūsic geweorþade,   wuldres Ealdor,
ēce Dryhten,   in ealle tīd.
                         Amen.

112–14. Corruption in these lines makes the sense irrecoverable. The most useful notes are those of Gordon, whom I have followed in the translation.

Blessed is he who humble lives; for grace
Shall come to him from heaven. The Creator
Shall make his spirit steadfast, for his faith
Is in God's might. Man must control himself
With strength of mind, and firmly hold to that,
True to his pledges, pure in all his ways.
With moderation should each man behave
In all his dealings with both friend and foe.
No man will wish the friend he's made to burn
In fires of hell, or on an earthly pyre,
Yet fate is mightier, the Lord's ordaining
More powerful than any man can know.
Let us think where we have our real home,
And then consider how we may come thither;
And let us labour also, so that we
May pass into eternal blessedness,
Where life belongs amid the love of God,
Hope in the heavens. The Holy One be thanked
That He has raised us up, the Prince of Glory,
Lord without end, to all eternity.

Amen.

The Whale

There is a group of three religious allegories in the Exeter Book which are all derived from a Latin version of *Physiologus*. They are *The Panther*, *The Whale*, and *The Partridge*. Owing to the loss of a leaf the last of these is almost wholly deficient. In the earliest versions the whale was in fact a turtle, to which ll. 8–10 of the present poem would be more appropriate. The Exeter Book also contains another rather similar though longer and more complex allegory in *The Phoenix*, which again ultimately derives from *Physiologus*, and for which see N. F. Blake, *The Phoenix*, Manchester, 1964. It is perhaps worth reflecting on the clarity with which the meaning of the allegory is presented in these poems when considering the more allegorical interpretations of such poems as *The Wanderer* and *The Seafarer*.

BIBLIOGRAPHY

ASPR III

Nū ic fitte gēn   ymb fisca cynn
wille wōðcræfte   wordum cȳþan
þurh mōdgemynd   bi þām miclan hwale.
Se bið unwillum   oft gemēted,
5 frēcne ond ferðgrim,   fareðlācendum,
niþþa gehwylcum;   þām is noma cenned,
fyrnstrēama geflotan,   Fastitocalon.
Is þæs hīw gelīc   hrēofum stāne,
swylce wōrie   bi wædes ōfre,
10 sondbeorgum ymbseald,   særȳrica mæst,
swā þæt wēnaþ   wæglīþende
þæt hȳ on ēalond sum   ēagum wlīten,
ond þonne gehȳdað   hēahstefn scipu
tō þām unlonde   oncyrrāpum,
15 setlaþ sæmēaras   sundes æt ende,
ond þonne in þæt ēglond   up gewītað
collenferþe;   cēolas stondað
bi staþe fæste,   strēame biwunden.
Ðonne gewīciað   wērigferðe,
20 faroðlācende,   frēcnes ne wēnað,
on þām ēalonde   æled weccað,
hēahfȳr ælað;   hæleþ bēoþ on wynnum,
rēonigmōde,   ræste geliste.
Þonne gefēleð   fācnes cræftig
25 þæt him þā fērend on   fæste wuniaþ,
wīc weardiað   wedres on luste,
ðonne semninga   on sealtne wæg
mid þā nōþe   niþer gewīteþ
gārsecges gæst,   grund gesēceð,

1. *fitte gen. The Whale* follows *The Panther* in the Exeter Book.

The Whale

Now will I in another song make known,
Reveal in words, with verse-craft, from my mind
About a race of fish, the mighty whale.
He often is found fierce and grim of heart,
Not by their wish, to travellers by sea,
To every man; this sailor of the sea-streams
Has got the name of Fastitocolon.
His countenance is like the rugged stone
As if the greatest mass of sea-weed lay
Beside the shore, with sand-banks all around,
So that the seafarers are made to think
That they look on some island with their eyes;
And then they fasten up their high-prowed ship
With cables on that land which is no land,
Tie the sea-horses at the water's edge,
And so onto the island up they go
In cheerful spirits, while their vessels stand
Fast by the shore, encircled by the currents.
Then weary-spirited the voyagers
Set up their camp, they have no thought of danger,
And on that island they start kindling flames,
Make a great fire; the heroes are in joy,
Though tired in spirit, longing for their rest.
Then, skilled in evil-doing, he perceives
The travellers are firmly settled on him,
Live in their camp delighting in good weather,
And suddenly into the salt sea wave
The creature of the ocean sinks with them
Rapidly downwards, visits the sea-bed,

30 ond þonne in dēaðsele   drence bifæsteð
    scipu mid scealcum.   Swā bið scinna þēaw,
    dēofla wīse,   þæt hī drohtende
    þurh dyrne meaht   duguðe beswīcað,
    ond on teosu tyhtaþ   tilra dǣda,
35 wēmað on willan,   þæt hȳ wrāþe sēcen,
    frōfre tō fēondum,   oþþæt hȳ fæste ðǣr
    æt þām wǣrlogan   wīc gecēosað.
    Þonne þæt gecnāweð   of cwicsūsle
    flāh fēond gemāh,   þætte fīra gehwylc
40 hæleþa cynnes   on his hringe biþ
    fæste gefēged,   hē him feorgbona
    þurh slīþen searo   siþþan weorþeð,
    wloncum ond hēanum,   þe his willan hēr
    firenum fremmað,   mid þām hē fǣringa,
45 heoloþhelme biþeaht,   helle sēceð,
    gōda gēasne,   grundlēasne wylm
    under mistglōme,   swā se micla hwæl,
    se þe bisenceð   sǣlīþende
    eorlas ond ȳðmēaras.   Hē hafað ōþre gecynd,
50 wæterþisa wlonc,   wrǣtlīcran gīen.
    Þonne hine on holme   hungor bysgað
    ond þone āglǣcan   ǣtes lysteþ,
    ðonne se mereweard   mūð ontȳneð,
    wīde weleras;   cymeð wynsum stenc
55 of his innoþe,   þætte ōþre þurh þone,
    sǣfisca cynn,   beswicen weorðaþ,
    swimmað sundhwate   þǣr se swēta stenc
    ūt gewīteð.   Hī þǣr in farað
    unware weorude,   oþþæt se wīda ceafl

---

45. *heoloþhelm* means 'a helmet which makes the wearer invisible'.

And in that hall of death sets ships and men
To drown. Such is the practice of the demons,
The way of devils, that by acting thus
By secret power they deceive the troop,
By fraud persuade them to renounce good deeds,
Wilfully tempt them so they sadly seek
Comfort from enemies, till in the end
They firmly choose their home with their betrayer.
When the deceitful wicked fiend perceives
By vivid torment that some humankind,
Some race of men, have firmly fixed themselves
In his dominions, then he makes himself
By cruel craft their slayer afterwards,
Who in their pride and arrogance perform
His will on earth with crime; suddenly then
With helmet on which hides him from men's sight,
Lacking in goodness he goes down to hell,
The baseless surge beneath the misty gloom,
Like the great whale which sinks the voyagers,
Both men and ships. He has another way,
That proud seafarer, yet more marvellous.
When hunger comes upon him in the sea
And the grim creature wishes to have food,
Then the sea-guardian opens up his mouth,
His gaping lips; a pleasant smell comes forth
From his insides, and by it other kinds
Of fishes of the sea become deceived
And, swift in swimming, go where the sweet smell
Emerges from him. Then they pass therein
In an unwary crowd, till the wide jaw

60 gefylled bið;   þonne fǣringa
    ymbe þā herehūþe   hlemmeð tōgædre
    grimme gōman.   Swā biþ gumena gehwām,
    se þe oftost his   unwærlīce
    on þās lǣnan tīd   līf biscēawað,
65 lǣteð hine beswīcan   þurh swētne stenc,
    lēasne willan,   þæt hē biþ leahtrum fāh
    wið Wuldorcyning.   Him se āwyrgda ongēan
    æfter hinsīþe   helle ontȳneð,
    þām þe lēaslīce   līces wynne
70 ofer ferhtgereaht   fremedon on unrǣd.
    Þonne se fǣcna   in þām fæstenne
    gebrōht hafað,   bealwes cræftig,
    æt þām edwylme   þā þe him on cleofiað,
    gyltum gehrodene,   ond ǣr georne his
75 in hira līfdagum   lārum hȳrdon,
    þonne hē þā grimman   gōman bihlemmeð
    æfter feorhcwale   fæste tōgædre,
    helle hlinduru;   nāgon hwyrft ne swice,
    ūtsīþ ǣfre,   þā þǣr in cumað,
80 þon mā þe þā fiscas   faraðlācende
    of þæs hwæles fenge   hweorfan mōtan.
    Forþon is eallinga   . . . .

    dryhtna Dryhtne,   ond ā dēoflum wiðsace
    wordum ond weorcum,   þæt wē Wuldorcyning
85 gesēon mōton.   Uton ā sibbe tō Him
    on þās hwīlnan tīd   hǣlu sēcan,
    þæt wē mid swā lēofne   in lofe mōtan
    tō wīdan fēore   wuldres nēotan.

82. There is no gap in the MS.

Is altogether filled; then suddenly
He shuts the grisly jaws together round
His booty; so it is for every man,
He who most often thinks about his life
Heedlessly in this transitory time,
Lets himself be deceived by the sweet smell,
The false desire, that he is stained by sin
Against the King of Glory. The accursed
Opens hell's gates after their going hence
For those who foolish gave themselves in sin
To fleshly joys rather than what is right.
When the malicious one, skilful in sin,
Has brought in those who used to call on him
To that safe place, that whirlpool of hot fire,
Loaded with guilt, and those who formerly
Keenly obeyed his orders in their lives,
Then he snaps shut the grisly jaws on them,
Firmly together the strong doors of hell
After their death; and those who come therein
Have no return, escape, or parting ever,
Just as the fish who swim upon the sea
Can never turn away from the whale's grasp.

· · · · · · · · ·

. . . The Lord of Lords, and ever fight the devil
With words and deeds, that we may see the King
Of Glory. Let us ever seek from Him
Peace and salvation in this passing time,
That we with Him so dear may live in bliss,
May dwell in glory to eternity.

Textual Variants

The following is a list of instances in which the printed texts vary from the MS readings, without acknowledgment to the proposers of these emendations, for which see the notes in *The Anglo-Saxon Poetic Records* or in the other detailed editions. No notice is given of MS word divisions. Some texts with a particularly complicated background are not included; for *The Fight at Finnsburh* see Klaeber; for *The Battle of Brunanburh* see Campbell; for *Durham, Preface* and *Epilogue to Pastoral Care, Cædmon's Hymn* and *Bede's Death Song*, see *ASPR*.
The reading in the text is given first.

The Ruin

4. hrungeat; hrim geat torras. 18. monade myne; -nade *and* m-*supplied* (Leslie, MS damaged). 26 secgrofra; secg rof. 33. gefrætwed; gefrætweð. 44. under; -der *supplied, MS damaged*. 45. oþþæt; o- *supplied, MS damaged*.

Battle of Maldon

20. randas; randan. 61. we; þe. 103. feohte; fohte. 109. grimme *supplied*. 113. wearð; weard. 116. wearð; wærd. 171. gestandan; gestundan. 173. Ic geþancie; geþance. 191. ærndon; ærdon. 192. Godwine; godrine. 200. modiglice; modelice. 201. þearfe; þære. 208. forlætan; forlætun. 212. Gemunað þara; gemunu þa. 224. ægðer; ægder. 297. forð ða; forða. 298. sunu; suna. 299 geþrange; geþrang. 324. oð; od. 325. guðe; gude.

Wife's Lament

15. her eard; herheard.   20. hycgendne; hycgende.   24. fornumen *supplied*.   25. Sceal; seal.   37. sittan; sittam.

Husband's Message

For ll. 1–7, 36–40, see Leslie and *ASPR*.
8. hafu; hofu.   9. sceal; scealt.   10. modlufan; modlufun.   21. læran; læram.   30. on *supplied*, gelimpan *supplied*.   33. þæt git *supplied*.   34. sinc brytnian *supplied, only* s *visible in MS*. 37. þæt he mid *supplied, only* d *visible*.   38. holdra; hold- *supplied*.   41. gelagu *supplied*. The MS is damaged at this point and I am indebted to Leslie for all proposals from 33 on.

Wulf and Eadwacer

16. earmne; earne.

Deor

14. mone; monge.   30. earfoða; earfoda.

Riddles

5.5 me; mec.   5.8 hondweorc; 7 weorc. (*7 was the standard abbrevia tion for* and/ond.   5.9. a bidan; abidan.   9.1 ofgeafun; ofgeafum. 9.3 an *supplied*.   9.4 þeccan; weccan.   9.6 swa arlice; snearlice. 11.2 minum *supplied*.   12.6 beorne; beorn.   14.14 on *supplied*. 14.17 wraþum; wraþþum.   21.4 se *supplied*.   21.7 bearwe; bearme. 26.6 ecg; ecge.   26.12 hyde; hyþe.   60.9 meodubence; meodu. 60.12 seaxes; seaxeð.   60.15 twam; twan.

Gnomic Verses

10. swutolost; swicolost.   16. helme; hellme.   19. earm; earn. 24. mencgan; mecgan.   40. of; on.

Charm 12

6. wolues; uolmes. 9. scerne; scesne.

Judith

47. ymbe; 7 ymbe. 62. gangan *supplied*. 85. þearfendre; þear-
ffendre. 87. heorte; heorte ys. 134. hie; hie hie. 144. Iudith;
iudithe. 165. þeodnes; þeoðnes. 179. starian; stariað. 201.
sigeþufas; þufas. 207. wiston; westan. 234. ricne; rice.
249. werigferhðe; weras ferhðe. 251. hilde; hyldo. 263. hæste;
hæfte. 266. dægweorce; dæge weorce. 287. nu *supplied*. 288. life
supplied. 333. on; 7.

The Dream of the Rood

2. hwæt; hæt. 9. engeldryhta feala; engel dryhtnes ealle. 15.
geweorðod; geweorðode. 17. bewrigen; bewrigene. Wealdendes;
wealdes. 20. sorgum; surgum. 47. ænigum; nænigum. 59. sorgum
supplied. 63. hine; hie. 70. greotende; reotende. 71. stefn;
syððan. 91. holtwudu; holmwudu. 117. anforht; unforht.
142. me; he.

The Wanderer

14. healde; healdne. 22. minne; mine. 24. waþema; waþena.
27. min *supplied*. 28. freondleasne; freondlease. 44. giefstoles;
giefstolas. 59. modsefa; modsefan. 64. weorþan; wearþan.
74. eall; ealle. 84. deorce; deornce. 102. hrusan; hrusc.

The Seafarer

25. hyrnednebba; urigfeþra. 26. frefran; feran. 49. wlitigiað;
wlitigað. 52. gewitan; gewitað. 55. bittre; bitter. 56. sefteadig;
eft eadig. 63. hwælweg; wælweg. 67. stondað; stondeð. 69. tid
age; tide ge. 72. biþ; þæt. 75. fremum; fremman. 79. blæd;
blæð. 82. nearon; næron. 109. mon; mod. 115. swiþre; swire.
117. *2nd* we; se.

The Whale

58. gewiteð; gewitað.